THE BIRDWATCHER'S COMPANION

Malcolm Tait
and
Olive Tayler

A THINK BOOK FOR

ROBSON BOOKS

In order to see birds it is necessary to become part of the silence

Robert Lynd

THINK

A Think Book
for Robson Books

First published in Great Britain in 2005 by
Robson Books
The Chrysalis Building, Bramley Road, London W10 6SP

An imprint of **Chrysalis** Books Group plc

Edited by Malcolm Tait and Olive Tayler
Companion team: Tilly Boulter, James Collins, Rhiannon Guy,
Emma Jones, Jo Swinnerton, Lou Millward Tait and Marcus Trower

Think Publishing
The Pall Mall Deposit
124-128 Barlby Road, London W10 6BL
www.thinkpublishing.co.uk

The Wildfowl & Wetlands Trust
Slimbridge, Gloucestershire GL2 7BT
www.wwt.org.uk

ISBN 1-86105-833-0

Printed in Italy

It is only by watching, studying and talking about birds in the field that we really get to know them.
There is no substitute for experience.

Bill Oddie

This book would not have been possible without the support and flights of fancy of the following:

Claire Ashton, David Chamberlain, Judy Darley, Mike Daw, Amshula Ghumman, Leigh Gold, Lois Lee, Matt Packer, Peter Tait and Nancy Waters

When I was young, I thought I'd never be a driver. I couldn't see how it would be possible. Driving is an act of concentration, requiring a constant focus on the horizon and below, hands free to do nothing but grip the wheel, fiddle with the radio, and move that gear thingy that makes the engine change noise. How could I possibly do all that, when I'd spent a childhood of car journeys staring out the window at the horizon and above, following distant specks until I could see them no more, distracted by every flutter in passing hedgerows, scanning motorway-side fields with shaking binoculars? How could I possibly drive when the only things that mattered on a journey were the birds I might encounter?

Well, I do drive, and so do millions of others just like me. But fellow road-users need not worry. They're quite safe. Birdwatchers are remarkable beings who have discovered ways of folding their passion into their everyday lives, just as (to shift gear from motoring to cooking) a chef blends a herb into a sauce; the sauce still comes good, but has a little extra flavour permeating through.

And there's no better flavour than the tang of birdwatching. Birders, 'dudes', twitchers or garden-watchers, we've all developed that peripheral vision for soaring, bobbing, gliding, pecking objects, that helps us to root occasions and events in our memory. Remember that visit to that abbey while the Queen was visiting and it snowed in June and we first drank Earl Grey tea? Er, no. Yes you do, it was where we saw some jackdaws mobbing a peregrine. Ah, THAT place.

Birds are the snippets of life that seep into our consciousness and form wheeling patterns of memory. We'd be lost without them. We'd have to reshape our view of the world and of our own lives, and we'd be much the poorer for that. This book is a celebration of those snippets; like those childhood car journeys it's a collection of random, fleeting glimpses of the avian kingdom, sometimes startling, sometimes amusing, sometimes uplifting. And you never know what you're going to see round the next bend.

Just promise me one thing: please don't read it while you're driving.

Malcolm Tait, Editor

In 2003, a quiz in a wildlife magazine included the question: which of the following is a bird – flamecrest, firecrest, smokecrest, ashcrest. Well, a bit of a trick question, actually (although possibly by mistake), for in addition to the firecrest, the flamecrest also exists, although in only a small part of the world. Endemic to the mountainous areas of Taiwan, the little 'crest is similar to its fiery and golden cousins, except chiefly for its broad white stripes around its eye which give it the impression of having a shiner, and for its slightly brighter crest.

But what is such a tiny creature doing so far away from its nearest relatives? It's believed that its ancestors first emerged in the Himalayas, spreading north, west and east, then south again during the ice age, spreading their range across Eurasia. The branch that reached Taiwan was probably cut off from the mainland, leaving the tiny flamecrest alone of its family. A sensitive bird, it nests and roosts in only a few species of conifer, and is one of the reminders that not all cold climate creatures need to be large.

In fact studies of its cousin the goldcrest in Scandinavia have revealed that these little birds have adapted astonishingly well to the cold. During an 18-hour period at temperatures around 25°C, they survived by fuelling themselves on their fat reserves, up to 20% of their body weight. And when you've only got a maximum of eight grams to play with in the first place, that's saying something.

QUOTE UNQUOTE

God loved the birds and invented trees.
Man loved the birds and invented cages.
Jacques Deval, screenwriter

THE STORIES BEHIND THE BIRDS OF HOLLYWOOD

Next time you feel like doing something ridiculous, go with the flow. You never know where it might lead. When Clarence Nash went on radio in the 1930s and read out Mary had a Little Lamb in the voice of the lamb, he must have thought it was an idiotic one-off. But listening at home was a young film-maker who, impressed by what he heard, asked Nash to come on over to his studio for a chat. The only thing was that the film-maker, Walt Disney, thought that he was listening to an impersonation of a duck, not a lamb. Nash simply shrugged, and went on to provide the voice of Donald Duck for more than 50 years until his death in 1985.

BIRDBRAINERS

Name that phrase:
I'll show you a Parus, you emblazon it on my shoulder
Answer on page 153

OOPS

Even the best make mistakes.
The following are real boo-boos made by experienced birders:

Thought it was	Actually was
Eagle	Heron
Stone curlew	Rabbit
Nightjar	Car alarm
Great northern diver	Mooing cow
Eagle owl	Plastic decoy
Almost anything	A pigeon

WINGED WORDS

Last winter a whooper swan flew into the high-voltage electricity lines that traverse our glen. Every winter these cables take a sorry toll of migratory swans. This one fell to the ground in a swampy field. Its wing was broken. The sharp bone protruded pale and bloody through the layers of white feathers like a broken timber. Its leg was badly twisted, probably broken too. It shuffled helplessly into a patch of rushes where it lay, blinking out at me the pathos of its own inevitable destruction. There is no effective cure for a swan's shattered wing – certainly none that would allow it to fly free and to return to the Arctic to breed. The leg simply made things worse. At this point no cruelty had occurred. An unhappy accident had befallen an unlucky swan. It was in great pain, I am in no doubt about that, although I am glad that it lacked the cerebral capacity to understand either what had befallen it or the terminal implications of its injuries. Its sad, oriental face tilted and pivoted on its elegant neck. All it knew was the fear of my presence and that it could not fly away. I gazed at its slightly gaping, black and yellow fluted bill. Clouds of dread drifted through its liquid eye, making me wince. Remorse flooded in. I wanted to reverse the clock and see it fly again in chevron formation with its seven fellow swans; my spirit longed for the rhythmic whoop of its wings and its wild bugling, summoning the beauty of the morning.

John Lister-Kaye, *Nature's Child: Encounters with Wonders of the Natural World,* 2004

There's barely a birdwatcher around who hasn't felt the sting of mild social opprobrium. Creeping around a wooded lane with a pair of binoculars and a look of intent is likely to draw suspicious glances, while most people's response to the announcement of your hobby is along the lines of: 'Birds, eh? I hope you mean the feathered kind'. But it wasn't always this way. There was a time when birdwatching was recognised as a social need, for without it, communities and even kingdoms could fail.

In ancient times, in many parts of the world, birds were seen as messengers of the gods. Their actions would reveal weather patterns and divine intervention, so shamans and augurs needed to understand the creatures in order to predict the future.

In Rome, for example, at times of war, seers would predict outcomes and even strategies by watching chickens. Depending on whether or not the chickens ate, and how much they ate, the seer would recommend attack or retreat. The hungrier the birds, the more successful the soldiers would be. The crow, meanwhile, according to both Horace and Virgil, was a predictor of rain, every time it called.

Although Roman augurs might well have been earning a living from old rope, weather prediction from the behaviour of birds is quite possible, and still exists today, particularly in the parts of the world with more extreme climatic conditions. The Maheshkhali islanders of Bangladesh, one of several groups of people increasingly affected by global warming, recognise the departure of arboreal birds from their island as a sign that cyclones are approaching.

The Yunga of Peru, meanwhile, watch carefully the flight of the pardela, or gull, to predict when their precious rains might fall.

In Zimbabwe, where rainfall is so important, local lore has it that when the quelea nests high in the trees, then this year's rain will be good. There's logic here. Queleas often nest in trees alongside riverbanks, so high rainfall might flood the river, and the predictive birds have got themselves out of harm's way.

Japan's Saigasaki people have a similar lore. Local swallows (tsubame) tend to nest on the second floor of buildings, but occasionally choose the third or even fourth floors, an indication that a typhoon, with its destructive low-level water flooding, is on its way. They've also noticed that various types of birds tend to eat more quickly when a typhoon is approaching.

Swan

Flying Bird

Goose

Your Guests

WHAT A GREAT VOICE

There's an old dictum while walking in the woods: if you hear a call and don't recognise it, it's probably a great tit. The standard 'teacher, teacher' call is well known, its sharp whistle carrying for great distances in the crisp spring air, but at least 80 variants and other calls have also been recorded.

This vocal range, which expands as the great tit gets older, has led to an interesting phenomenon in the urban world. In order to be heard above traffic and other city sounds, great tits in such locations call and sing louder than their rural counterparts. Current research suggests that other birds without the great tit's repertoire and learning power may not be able to develop the same ability.

Maximum weight, in grams, of the marsh tit 13

FALLING FAST

The Common Birds Census and the Breeding Bird Survey have provided in recent years the strongest indicators of population trends of British birds. During the period 1970–2001, the most disastrous population falls among 100 widespread species that these surveys have revealed are:

Tree sparrow	94% decline
Lesser redpoll	89% decline
Corn bunting	89% decline
Woodcock	87% decline
Grey partridge	86% decline
Willow tit	85% decline
Spotted flycatcher	82% decline
Turtle dove	77% decline
Lesser spotted woodpecker	77% decline
Tree pipit	68% decline

A BARN OWL BY ANY OTHER NAME

Regional names for Tyto alba:
Berthuan (Cornwall)
Billy Wise (Norfolk)
Cherubim (Northamptonshire)
Moggy (Sussex)
Pudge (Leicestershire)
Ullat (Yorkshire)

BIRDS YOU MIGHT MYTH

If you should come across the Amazonian shrine to Ares on an island deep in the Black Sea, the best advice is to duck, or make sure you have your full set of armour to hand. The shrine is guarded by a flock of birds that, as Jason and his Argonauts discovered, give a new meaning to feather-touch. The birds, or Ornithes Areos, are able to fire their feathers which can pierce flesh, like arrows. The Argonauts had the answer, however: they set their helmets on their heads, and while half the company rowed, the remainder raised their shields for protection, roofing the ship 'as a man roofs his house with firmly fitted overlapping tiles', all of them shouting throughout the journey. As the feathery darts bounced harmlessly away, the yelling men were able to beach the Argo on the island, where they began to clatter their spears against their shields, and the birds, full of confusion, beat a hasty retreat.

14 *Number of potatoes per hour a human would have to eat to match the energy of a hummingbird*

Close to our bows, strange forms in the water darted hither and thither before us; while thick in our rear flew the inscrutable sea-ravens. And every morning, perched on our stays, rows of these birds were seen; and spite of our hootings, for a long time obstinately clung to the hemp, as though they deemed our ship some drifting, uninhabited craft; a thing appointed to desolation, and therefore fit roosting-place for their homeless selves. And heaved and heaved, still unrestingly heaved the black sea, as if its vast tides were a conscience; and the great mundane soul were in anguish and remorse for the long sin and suffering it had bred.

Herman Melville, *Moby Dick, 1851*

ALL FRIGATES GREAT OR SMALL

Great tit – *Parus major*. Great spotted woodpecker – *Dendrocopos major*. Makes sense, but try this: the greater frigatebird is *Fregata minor* (the lesser frigatebird being *Fregata ariel*). Why? The bird's original generic name was *Pelecanus*, and when it was reclassified it followed standard taxonomic practice of precedence, and retained its specific name.

PAYBACK FOR THE PAYCOCK

As the eagle is the bird of Jupiter, so the peacock is the bird of Juno, and it was this association that Sean O'Casey played with in his 1929 play *Juno and the Paycock*, the story of a Dublin family for whom pretty much everything goes wrong.

The Paycock is Captain Boyle, so nicknamed for his strutting walk. He's not really a captain, titling himself so thanks to a single sea trip. Boyle calls his wife Juno, as she 'was born and christened in June. I met her in June; we were married in June'. Their son Johnny has been crippled by a bullet he received during Easter 1916, while daughter Mary is trying to read herself out of the life she leads. Unfortunately, she falls in with a bad lot, a law student who leads the family to believe they are to inherit a fortune. The Boyles spend like crazed souls, only to find that the student has actually bungled the will, leaving them with nothing... and Mary with a baby. Johnny, meanwhile, has betrayed a comrade to the authorities. His old group catch up with him, and Mrs Boyle is called by the police to come and identify the body.

Throughout the catalogue of disasters, the Paycock remains gloriously drunk. He gets to speak the fitting final words of the play: 'The whole world's in a terrible state of chaos'. Go see the play. It'll cheer you up no end.

YOU CAN'T HAVE A BIRD
BOOK WITHOUT PARROT JOKES

Man buys a parrot and brings him home. As soon as they're indoors, the parrot launches into a stream of invective that would make a sailor blush. For five whole minutes he keeps it up, without even repeating himself once, until the man can take it no more and throws the bird into a cupboard. It doesn't do any good. There's banging and crashing going on like nothing else and, fearing complaints from the neighbours, the man opens the cupboard door and out flies the bird, cursing and effing and blinding like never before.

It's all too much. The man grabs him by the scruff of the neck and chucks him into the freezer to cool him off. Once again with the banging and crashing until... suddenly, all goes silent. Worrying that the bird might be injured, the man opens the freezer door, and the parrot steps meekly out onto his arm.

'Awfully sorry about all that vile language back there', says the bird. 'Word of honour, I'll do my best to improve my manners. One question though, and pardon me for asking, but what did the chicken do?'

QUOTE UNQUOTE

*'I know'd my name to be Magwitch, chrisen'd Abel.
How did I know it? Much as I know'd the birds'
names in the hedges to be chaffinch, sparrer, thrush. I
might have thought it was all lies together, only as the
birds' names come out true, I supposed mine did.'*
Magwitch, in Charles Dickens' *Great Expectations*

AN EYE FOR AN OWL

The furthering of ornithological research through a variety of media is the aim of the Eric Hosking Trust, which offers bursaries for projects as varied as Bali Starling Research and short stories about birds for young people. It was founded in 1991 in memory of perhaps the best bird photographer ever to have clicked a shutter.

Yet the Trust might never have existed. Hosking, when just 27, was trying to film a tawny owl at its nest, when 'out of the silent darkness a swift and heavy blow struck my face. There was an agonising stab in my left eye. I could see nothing. The owl, with its night vision, had dive-bombed with deadly accuracy, sinking a claw deep into the centre of my eye'. Infection set in, and his eye was removed to save the other one. Despite his monocular vision, Hosking was able to continue his career.

A 950-word vocabulary is one thing; the ability to use the words in context is something else. N'kisi, an African grey parrot living in New York, appears to have both, and as a result, controversy is not far behind.

Animal behaviourists, parrot-fanciers (psittacologists?) and anyone else with an interest in human-style animal communication have been debating the creativity of N'kisi for years. He appears to know the difference between past, present and future tenses; he forms compound word structures to describe situations for which he does not have vocabulary; he seems at times to know what his owner is thinking; he even appears to have a sense of humour. When introduced to Jane Goodall, the chimpanzee guru whose picture with the apes he had already seen, he asked 'Got a chimp?' When shown aromatherapy oils, he called them 'pretty smell medicine'. The debate is: does he consciously create meanings using the vocabulary he has been taught, or is it humans who are reading something extra into a large but simple arrangement of verbal signs?

Whatever the truth behind his animal brain, he comes across as a wry old thing. He was once sitting next to another parrot, which decided to hang upside-down from its perch. N'kisi's comment? 'You got to put this bird on the camera.'

ALPHA, BETA, GREBA

The dabchick and its relations are the only birds in the English-speaking world to contain consecutively the letters 'a, b, c'. Just thought you ought to know that.

10 SURE SIGNS YOU WATCH BIRDS

1. You view a friend's personality change as 'new behaviour'.
2. You're sure the first four letters of 'telescope' are silent.
3. Your children's middle names are Ardea and Tyto.
4. You've been to a couple of village cricket matches but never seen a wicket fall.
5. You have an extra couple of creases in the back of your neck.
6. You wonder why Doctor Dolittle wasted his precious gift on dogs, chimps and pushme-pullyous.
7. You own an original Lars Jonsson.
8. In one way or another, warblers represent the best times of your life and the worst.
9. You always park in the same spot at the Bird Fair.
10. You ask an usher to check your pager on your wedding day.

BUT DO THEY SERVE KESTREL?

Of the 50 commonest pub names in Britain, birds only feature in two, and even then, it's the same bird. The Swan is the fourth most likely name you'll come across, while at number 43 sits The White Swan. Nonetheless, there are some more unusual pub signs bearing avian monikers, as this list attests:

The Sociable Plover in Portsmouth
The Drunken Duck in Hawkshead
The Strawbury Duck in Entwhistle
The Falcon and Firkin in London
The Quaggy Duck in London
The Fox and Pelican in Hindhead
The Crow and Gate in Crowborough
The Orange Pelican in Letchworth
The Parrot and Punchbowl in Aldringham
The Take a Gander in Burringham
The Dove and Rainbow in Sheffield
The Parrot and Alligator in Bourton-on-the-Water
The Ducks Don't Float in Evesham

QUOTE UNQUOTE

*It is an irony that the very strangeness and beauty of the wild
and unfamiliar can be destroyed by the observation of it.*
Olive Tait, writer and gardener

CROWNING GLORY

The maternal instinct in birds is indefatigable, right? Wrong, according to the Netherlands Institute of Ecology at the Centre of Terrestrial Ecology. The Institute's recent study of breeding blue tits suggested that females with less handsome mates make less of an effort to rear their young.

Now, handsome is as handsome does, and in the case of the blue tit, it seems that the males with the brightest UV colouration on their crown feathers are the most desirable. When researchers, who worked with pairs that had already mated, applied sunscreen to these feathers, blocking out the UV colouration, the females seemed to lose interest in the family they were about to raise. They visited the nest less frequently, and brought less food, resulting in weaker chicks.

'It's the first time such behaviour adjustment has been shown,' said Tobias Limbourg who led the research. He also added, rather controversially: 'If a similar study was carried out on humans, I would assume that human mothers would show the same preferential treatment.' Best not go there, Tobias.

COME FOR THE BIRDS.
STAY FOR THE SHRIMPS

If you think that a visit to a Wildfowl & Wetlands Trust is all about birds, think again. Not only do the country's nine reserves play host to a wealth of mammal, insect and plantlife, one of them is home to one of the oldest living creatures on the planet.

It's the tadpole shrimp, which was discovered alive and well at the WWT's Scottish reserve at Caerlaverock near Dumfries in 2004. Only the second UK population of this ancient creature, (the other one is in the New Forest), the Caerlaverock crustaceans have suddenly appeared, perhaps because their eggs had lain dormant in the mud for decades.

And just how old are they? Older than the dinosaurs. Fossils show that they were around at least 220 million years ago, and have not changed in appearance since. And to think we use 'shrimp' as a derogatory term!

SONGS THAT WERE NEARLY ABOUT BIRDS

Dirty Linnet, Fairport Convention
Ain't a-gonna Grebe, Bob Dylan
DJ Vulture, Pet Shop Boys
Be My Plover, Alice Cooper
Daddy Coot, Boney M
Magpie May, Rod Stewart
Poison Sparrow, ABC
Yellow Hammerine, Beatles

THE CRYING BIRD

The limpkin, a heron-like bird of the Florida swamps and southern America, gains its name from its slow undulating gait and clumsy flight, but holds more remarkable claims to fame. The sole member of its family, and possibly a link between the cranes and the rails, it emits a call that ranks with that of the great northern diver for its eeriness. In fact, it's more of a shriek than a call, and was believed by the early pioneers to be the screams of tortured souls of the dead who lay in the swamps. It is also given the name of crying bird.

In fact, it is believed by some peoples of the Amazon that when the limpkin starts calling, the rivers will cease to rise. Such reverence for the bird is unsurprising once you've heard the desperate quality of the call, which has been described variously as 'little children lost in the swamps for ever'; 'a hoarse rattling cry like the gasp of a person being strangled'; and 'an unearthly shriek with the quality of unutterable sadness'.

The Rajasthan desert gives way to neem and khejri savanna, and as this is a Vishnoi region where wild things pass undisturbed, small herds of nilgai, sometimes attended by demoiselle cranes, are now quite common. Though these big antelope look clumsy with their humps and their small heads, they can outrun the tiger and lion that used to abound in this region. Today the lion is entirely gone from Rajasthan, and the tiger is confined to scattered enclaves such as the maharajah of Jaipur's former hunting tract at Ranthambore, where we are headed.

Along the road goes a white-robed party of Jain monks and nuns, and a man riding an elephant, and young girls with gold rings in their left nostrils, and a bride-to-be escorted on foot under a canopy woven of every colour of the sun, bound for a very different sort of wedding from the one we will witness this evening at the grand hotel in Jaipur – an immense ceremony on an artificial stage in the formal gardens, under the burning eye of a tiny spotted owlet that flies in out of the dark to perch on a lamppost and cock its head, glaring askance at this immense disruption of the night.

Peter Matthiessen, *The Birds of Heaven: Travels with Cranes*, 2001

BIRDBRAINERS

What do *Columba junionae* and *Glaucidium hardyi*
have in common with bowler hats?
Answer on page 153

WHAT'S IN A NAME?

To give someone a ducking, ie to submerge them in water, is a term that would appear to have come from the name of the bird. Yet in all likelihood, the derivation is the other way round. The Old English *duce* means 'one who ducks', which probably replaced the previous term for the bird, *ened*, which linked to the same Latin root that gives us the family name *Anatidae*.

Once the 'duck' had been accepted, possibly in the 14th century, it soon spawned a host of side-meanings: its use as a term of endearment first appeared in 1590, while the game of ducks-and-drakes, skipping stones across water, cropped up in 1583. The lame duck, a stock-exchange term, was coined in 1761, while 1908 saw the introduction of duck soup as slang for a thing easily accomplished.

Unsurprisingly, Henry VIII had his own meaning for the word, and equally unsurprisingly, it reflected his oft-horny mood. Writing to Anne Boleyn in about 1536, he referred to her breasts as those 'pritty duckys I trust shortly to kysse'.

In 1962 Rachel Carson, a novelist with environmental interests, published *Silent Spring*, a book often regarded as the launch of the environmental movement. Its title came from its content: keep using chemicals, and in time we will no longer hear the songbirds. It echoed the line from John Keats' *La Belle Dame Sans Merci*: 'the sedge is wither'd from the lake / And no birds sing'.

Like most novelists who step outside fiction to draw attention to the plight of the world (Arundhati Roy, for example), Carson was mocked and criticised by those who stood to lose most, in this case the chemical giants. One such critic was Dr William Darby, chairman of the department of biochemistry and director, division of nutrition, at Vanderbilt University school of medicine, who laid into not only the book, but its readers. 'Its bulk will appeal to those readers who are as uncritical as the author,' he wrote of its list of principal sources, 'or to those who find the flavour of her product to their taste. Those consumers will include the organic gardeners, the antifluoride leaguers, the worshippers of "natural foods", those who cling to the philosophy of a vital principle, and pseudo-scientists and faddists.'

Well, the 'faddists' won. DDT, the main target of the book, was subsequently outlawed as a pesticide, and *Silent Spring* itself became the ecologists' bible through the 70s and 80s.

Rachel Carson herself, however, did not fare so well. She died of cancer two years after the book's publication.

ON THE UP AND UP

The Common Birds Census and the Breeding Bird Survey have provided in recent years the strongest indicators of population trends of British birds. During the period 1970–2001, the most successful population increases among 100 widespread species that these surveys have revealed are:

Collared dove	345% increase
Buzzard	318% increase
Mute swan	192% increase
Great spotted woodpecker	185% increase
Blackcap	126% increase
Reed warbler	123% increase
Little grebe	118% increase
Nuthatch	115% increase
Green woodpecker	115% increase
Mallard	115% increase

THE WORLD'S 17 SPECIES OF PENGUIN

Species	Breeding pairs
Adelie	2,500,000
African	70,000
Chinstrap	7,500,000
Emperor	220,000
Erect-crested	170,000
Fjordland	3,000
Galapagos	1,000
Gentoo	320,000
Humboldt	12,000
King	2,000,000
Little, or Blue	500,000
Macaroni	9,000,000
Magellanic	1,800,000
Rockhopper	1,800,000
Royal	850,000
Snares	30,000
Yellow-eyed	1,500

THE STORIES BEHIND THE BIRDS OF HOLLYWOOD

The launch of the first Harry Potter film in 2001 led to an avalanche of calls being put through to birds of prey centres up and down the country. Literally hundreds of children wanted their own Hedwig for Christmas, and their gullible parents tried to get one for them. Because barn owls have a pale demeanour, rather like the snowy owl of the film, some breeders actually started offering them at 25 quid a head.

Worried that the birds would suffer once the craze wore off (rather like the terrapin-buying frenzy during Teenage Mutant Ninja Turtle fervour, or the dalmation spree when 101 of them appeared on the big screen), the message went out: an owl is for life, not just for Christmas. Interest then switched from ownership to sponsorship, and adopting owls in bird of prey centres became the preferred way of 'owning' the birds.

Meanwhile, in the States, an enterprising group called Defenders of Wildlife found another way to make the most of Pottermania. With an overall agenda of saving the Alaskan National Wildlife Refuge from President Bush's swaggering oil-drilling chums, they adopted the snowy owl as a symbol and gained excellent media coverage for their cause by encouraging children everywhere to 'save Hedwig'.

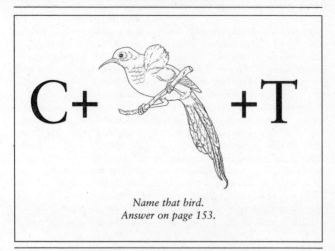

C+ +T

*Name that bird.
Answer on page 153.*

GOOSEY GOOSEY GANDER,
WHITHER SHALL YOU WANDER

How far do birds travel to moult? A few miles? Just up the road? The nearest lake?

Try 800 miles, round trip. A 2004 study of greylag geese by the Wildfowl & Wetlands Trust showed that the flock, based in Gloucestershire, flew all the way up to Glasgow to shed their plumage, returning to the West Country once their new feathers had grown. Why they choose to fly so far when there are eminently suitable sites near home, however, is still a mystery.

WHAT A LARK

Dunlin	Once known as sea lark in Cheshire
Sanderling	Once known as sea lark in Ireland
Ringed plover	Once known as sand lark in Northumberland
Common sandpiper	Once known as sand lark in Scotland
Corn bunting	Once known as horse lark in Cornwall
Yellowhammer	Once known as scribbling lark in Northamptonshire
Meadow pipit	Once known as titlark in Herefordshire
Rock pipit	Once known as dusky lark in Yorkshire

*NB: the yellowhammer got its name from the marks
on its egg, resembling a child's first drawings.*

Length, in centimetres, of the legs of a black-winged stilt. This represents 60% 23
of its overall height

Next to the dead the most numerous things on [Salisbury] Plain are sheep, rooks, pewits and larks. Today they mingle their voices, but the lark is the most constant. Here, more than elsewhere, he rises up above an earth only less free than the heavens. The pewit is equally characteristic. His winter and twilight cry expresses for most men both the sadness and the wildness of these solitudes. When his spring cry breaks every now and then, as it does today, through the songs of the larks, when the rooks caw in low flight or perched on their elm tops, and the lambs bleat, and the sun shines, and the couch fires burn well, and the wind blows their smoke about, the Plain is genial, and the unkindly breadth and simplicity of the scene in winter or in the drought of summer are forgotten.

Edward Thomas, *In Pursuit of Spring,* **1914**

QUOTE UNQUOTE

The early bird gets the worm, but the second mouse gets the cheese.
Anon

BORN TO LOVE BIRDS

There are many thousand species of dicky bird around the world, but a handful of them are slightly different. They're more properly known as dickey birds.

Donald Ryder Dickey (1887–1932) was an American naturalist who during his short life built an extraordinary collection of 50,000 wildlife specimens, now in various museums. As he became older, however, his records of creatures moved more towards the photographic, and his work, particularly on birds, became staple to the research conducted by the Smithsonian Institute.

It was a weak heart that finally killed him, but which also inflamed his passion for birds and mammals as a young man. 'During the two years I spent in bed,'

he wrote in 1926, 'after my pump played out in senior year, my idea of values underwent a change. I had always been keen about the out-of-doors, but had never expected to make more than a hobby of it. When I began to get my strength back after my long siege, I therefore started studying and photographing birds and mammals simply as a resource in time of need. Due to luck and an out-door life, I awoke about 1916 to find myself a thoroughly husky individual, but too interested by that time in what started as a hobby, to forgo it for a conventional business life.'

The Dickey quail, *Egretta rufescens dickeyi* (an egret) and *Icterus graduacauda dickeyae* (an oriole) are among those that bear his name.

The creation of the wild creatures, according to the Yaqui people of Mexico

A great bird lived on the hill of Otam Kawi. Every morning he would fly out in search of food. He caught men, women and children and carried them back to Otam Kawi to eat. In those days the people always were watchful. They couldn't have fiestas because when they did, two or three of the people were carried away by the big bird.

There was an old man who earned his livelihood by hunting deer. He did nothing else. He had only one daughter. She was big with a child who was soon to be born, when the bird carried away her husband. The baby, a boy, came in the afternoon.

The next year the bird carried away the mother, and the grandfather brought the child up on cow's milk. There were cows in those days, but no animals of the claw. This little boy never grew very big. When he was ten, he was still very small.

One afternoon he was seated outside of the house and he said, 'I have no mother'. 'Ah,' said the grandfather, 'The big bird carried her away. First he took your father, then your mother.'

'Where is that bird? I am going to grow up and kill that bird.' The old man laughed.

One day the boy went about alone, walking through the monte and looking up into the sky. There is a level plain east of Potam called maretabo'oka'apo. There the little boy walked. He had been hunting for three days. Then he saw the bird. Quickly he jumped into a hole. The big bird sat down in a mesquite tree, waiting for him to come out of the hole. The boy stayed there all day, watching the big bird in the mesquite tree. He saw everything; the size, the colours of the feathers, the big eyes. At night he went farther back in the hole and fell asleep. Late at night he awoke. The bird had gone with the coming of night.

Three days later, the boy returned to his home. His grandfather asked, 'My son, where have you been?'

'Over in the hills.'

'Weren't you afraid of the big bird?'

The little boy said, 'I saw him. I saw all of his coloured feathers and his big eyes. I climbed into a hole. I return only to ask permission to kill the bird. This bow would never kill him. It is too little. I wish you would make me one of that wood called kunwo. And I need another kind of arrow, made of wo'i baka. I will go as soon as you make me these'.

The grandfather made them for him, and the next day, before dawn, the boy left for Otam Kawi. All day long the boy waited. At last he saw the bird come in and alight in a large tree. Night fell and the bird went to sleep. Then the boy softly approached the tree. He measured twenty-five feet from the foot of the mesquite tree toward the west. There he made a deep hole, ten feet deep. When dawn came, he was still hunting poles and branches with which to cover it.

The bird saw him and was angry. The boy went down into the hole. He prepared his bow well. The bird came down from the mesquite tree and went to the hole. The boy was inside, looking out. He shot the big bird in the eye with an arrow.

The bird flew to the top of the mesquite tree. The boy shot three more arrows. The bird fell.

For a long time the boy did not come out of the hole. He waited to be sure that the bird was dead. When he was sure, he came out and went over to the big dead bird.

He pulled out a handful of its feathers and threw them into the air and the feathers became owls. With another handful of feathers he made smaller owls. With four handfuls of feathers, he made four classes of owls.

In the same way, with other handfuls of feathers, he made birds of every kind, crows and roadrunners. He threw the feathers and they became birds of different colours.

When he had finished all of the feathers, he cut off a piece of meat from the dead bird. He threw this and it became a mountain lion. He cut three more pieces and made three other kinds of big cat. After that he made four smaller kinds of cats.

With more meat the boy made foxes and raccoons and coyotes. He made snakes and all kinds of animals that have claws. Then he started home. He arrived there in two days. He came in very happily, dressed in a suit of feathers he had made from the bird, and he wore four feathers in his hat, two on either side.

He entered and his grandfather was frightened to see him covered with blood from the meat of the animal.

The old man was afraid, and he said, 'What happened to you?'

'I killed the big bird. Now you may walk about the world.'

THAT NAME IS MINE

Towards the end of the second world war, a series of paddle minesweepers was commissioned by the Admiralty as part of the nation's war defences. It was called the Bird Class, and there were six planned altogether, each named after a bird. When the war ended, the plans were mothballed, and paddle minesweepers HMS Fulmar, HMS Gadwall, HMS Pochard, HMS Stormy Petrel, HMS Redshank and HMS Shrike were never to be.

But the tradition of naming minesweepers in this way has continued. US coastal minesweepers have been given avian names for many years, dozens being churned out from Albatross to Waxbill. There have even been a couple called Bobolink.

The 15 species of crane are among the most endangered birds in the world, many of them still suffering falling populations. Estimations of their populations in the late 1990s, in descending order, were:

Sandhill Crane	520,000
Eurasian Crane	220,000–250,000
Demoiselle Crane	200,00–240,000
Brolga	Up to 100,000
Grey Crowned Crane	85,000–95,000
Black Crowned Crane	66,500–77,500
Blue Crane	21,000
Sarus Crane	13,500–15,500
Wattled Crane	13,000–15,000
Hooded Crane	9400–9600
Black-necked Crane	5600–6000
White-naped Crane	4900–5300
Siberian Crane	2900–3000
Red-crowned Crane	1700–2000
Whooping Crane	296

QUOTE UNQUOTE

There are only two or three human stories, and they go on repeating themselves as fiercely as if they had never happened before; like the larks in this country, that have been singing the same five notes over for thousands of years.
Willa Cather, writer

BIRDS YOU MIGHT MYTH

According to Mayan religious history, birds played a seminal role in the gods' first stab at creating mankind. Having made the earth, and the various animals upon it, the gods set about making men and women out of wood. The trouble was that these manikins had minds and spirits of their own, and treated the gods irreverently. The gods decided to start afresh, but first they had to deal with their original creations, which they did by sending the four birds of destruction down to earth. These birds certainly lived up to their name: first Xecotcovach tore out the manikins' eyes, then Camulatz cut off their heads. Cotzbalarn followed up by devouring their flesh, and Tecumbalam finished the job by grinding their bones and sinews into powder.

Some of the manikins got away, however, and their descendants are the monkeys that live hopefully alongside mankind today.

LOONAR TAKE-OFF

Alone among the diver (or loon, in the US) family, the red-throated is able to take off from land. For the rest, a pretty long watery runway is needed, the great northern diver in particular needing hundreds of feet to thrash along before it can get itself airborne. In fact, when conditions are calm and there's minimal wind speed for the bird to run into, a diver take-off can last for about a quarter of a mile.

BIRDBRAINERS

Who am I?
My first is in hawk but never in dove
My second's in raptor that you see above
My third is in balmy, the weather I need
My fourth is in double-quick, for that's my speed
My fifth's in the sky where I'm at my leisure
My whole is a pastime that gives you much pleasure
Answer on page 153

WINGED WORDS

I was going, today, by the side of a plat of ground, where there was a very fine flock of turkeys. I stopped to admire them, and observed to the owner how fine they were, when he answered, 'We owe them entirely to you, sir, for we never raised one till we read your *Cottage Economy*'. I then told him that we had, this year, raised two broods at Kensington, one black and one white, one of nine and one of eight; but that, about three weeks back, they appeared to become dull and pale about the head; and that, therefore, I sent them to a farmhouse, where they recovered instantly, and the broods being such a contrast to each other in point of colour, they were now, when prowling over a grass field, amongst the most agreeable sights that I had ever seen. I intended, of course, to let them get their full growth at Kensington, where they were in a grass plat about fifteen yards square, and where I thought that the feeding of them, in great abundance with lettuces and other greens from the garden, together with grain, would carry them on to perfection. But I found that I was wrong; and that though you may raise them to a certain size in a small place and with such management, they then, if so much confined, begin to be sickly. Several of mine began actually to droop: and the very day they were sent to the country, they became as gay as ever, and in three days all the colour about their heads came back to them.

William Cobbett,
Rural Rides, 1825

SO THE BIBLE WAS RIGHT?

And the Israelites went out into the wilderness, and there they feasted mightily on quail, the Bible tells us. Poor guys: soon afterwards they were hit by a plague.

An early conservation morality tale? Apparently not. Coturnism is a very unpleasant illness, very occasionally even fatal, that can be derived from eating the wild European quail, (genus *Coturnix*). Vomiting, breathing problems, great pain and even paralysis are among the discomforting symptoms, which can take up to a week to run through the body. For some years, it was believed that the toxicity was passed from the bird to people because quail eat hemlock seeds during migration, but as the plant is not in seed at this time more recent theories lean towards a diet of seeds of a species of mint, which is in seed at this time.

The problem only arises very rarely, and even then only when wild migrating quail is eaten. But with the bird in decline across Europe, partly due to hunting, perhaps coturnism, which has occurred in recent years in Algeria, Russia, Greece and Turkey, could become its salvation.

TOP 5 EUROPEAN BREEDING POPULATIONS OF BARN OWLS

Spain	Approx 66,000 pairs
France	Approx 30,000 pairs
Germany	Approx 10,000 pairs
Italy	Approx 10,000 pairs
Britain	Approx 4,000 pairs

ABSOLUTELY FABULOUS

The Eagle and the Jackdaw, by Aesop

An eagle, flying down from his perch on a lofty rock, seized upon a lamb and carried him aloft in his talons. A jackdaw, who witnessed the capture of the lamb, was stirred with envy and determined to emulate the strength and flight of the eagle. He flew around with a great whir of his wings and settled upon a large ram, with the intention of carrying him off, but his claws became entangled in the ram's fleece and he was not able to release himself, although he fluttered with his feathers as much as he could. The shepherd, seeing what had happened, ran up and caught him. He at once clipped the Jackdaw's wings, and taking him home at night, gave him to his children. On their saying, 'Father, what kind of bird is it?' he replied, 'To my certain knowledge he is a daw; but he would like you to think an eagle.'

Accept yourself for what you are

Up before the beak

SHOCKING STATE IN SERBIA

Poaching of birds in Serbia has reached titanic proportions in recent years, and most of the results end up on plates in European restaurants. As lark's tongues, nightingale pâté and roasted thrush gain popularity in Italy, Germany and even Belgium, so the birds disappear at an even greater rate from the Serbian ancient woodlands and nature reserves.

The statistics are frightening. The Serbian Society for the Protection of Birds has calculated that not one single breeding species in the country is increasing its population, while several have fallen by 80% in just the last decade. One lorry was stopped carrying 1,000kg of dead birds, while another was pulled over at Italian customs and found to contain a staggering 120,000 of the frozen little corpses.

And yet in all this time, not a single poacher, nor any of the government, police or customs officials who are also lining their pockets through the illicit trade, has been taken to court.

DOESN'T COUNT

The list of British species, according to the British Ornithologists' Union, would be 17 species longer if it could be proven that those species had occurred in a natural state. There is reasonable doubt that they did, however, so until further notice, the following birds have yet to make it to the official list, and sit in the no-bird's land of category D.

Falcated duck *Anas falcata*
Baikal teal *Anas formosa*
Marbled duck *Marmaronetta angustirostris*
Great white pelican *Pelecanus onocrotalus*
Greater flamingo *Phoenicopterus ruber*
Bald eagle *Haliaeetus leucocephalus*
Monk vulture *Aegypius monachus*
Egyptian vulture *Neophron percnopterus*
Saker falcon *Falco cherrug*
Asian brown flycatcher *Muscicapa dauurica*
Mugimaki flycatcher *Ficedula mugimaki*
Daurian starling *Sturnus sturninus*
White-winged snowfinch *Montifringilla nivalis*
Palm warbler *Dendroica palmarum*
Chestnut bunting *Emberiza rutila*
Red-headed bunting *Emberiza bruniceps*
Blue grosbeak *Passerina caerulea*

QUOTE UNQUOTE

Kestrels would be a much commoner sight in the London sky if gazing upwards were not such a dangerous occupation in London's traffic-laden streets.
RSR Fitter, naturalist and Londoner, 1945

THE VOICE OF THE TURTLE

Birdwatchers of a certain age will remember Percy Edwards who made a pretty decent living in the 1970s from popping up on radio and TV shows, performing his bird impressions. Audiences would sit and marvel as he performed his chiffchaff followed rapidly by a great tit, before rattling off a scolding blackbird call. A keen ornithologist, he could perform over 600 different calls.

But there was a Hollywood side to Percy too. His was the voice behind the eponymous characters in the films *The Plague Dogs* and *Orca*. And if the next time you're watching *Alien* you find yourself getting a bit tense, relax yourself by asking just how scary a chest-bursting, man-eating, shadow-skulking alien called Percy can really be.

Birds as observed by Gilbert White in his
Natural History of Selborne, 1788/9

On the thirteenth of April I went to the sheep-down, where the ring-ousels have been observed to make their appearance at spring and fall, in their way perhaps to the north or south; and was much pleased to see three birds about the usual spot. We shot a cock and a hen; they were plump and in high condition. The hen had but very small rudiments of eggs within her, which proves they are late breeders; whereas those species of the thrush kind that remain with us the whole year have fledged young before that time. In their crops was nothing very distinguishable, but somewhat that seemed like blades of vegetables nearly digested. In autumn they feed on haws and yew-berries, and in the spring on ivy-berries. I dressed one of these birds, and found it juicy and well-flavoured. It is remarkable that they make but a few days' stay in their spring visit, but rest near a fortnight at Michaelmas. These birds, from the observations of three springs and two autumns, are most punctual in their return; and exhibit a new migration unnoticed by the writers, who supposed they never were to be seen in any of the southern counties.

JUST ELEVEN TO GO

There are still 11 species, other than game birds, that do not enjoy the full protection of the law in England, each being on general licence, allowing authorised people to kill them if they are causing damage or spreading disease:

Carrion crow • Rook • Jay • Jackdaw • Magpie
Feral pigeon • Woodpigeon • Collared dove • Herring gull
Lesser black-backed gull • Great black-backed gull

THERE'S ALWAYS SOMEONE GROUSING

As reports come through on an almost daily basis of various threats to the world's birds, it's easy to forget that we have nonetheless come a long way in the last few decades. Even as recently as the mid-60s, a forestry handbook listed five species as 'definitely harmful'. The woodpigeon and jay are still classified as potential pests, but two others now enjoy full protection: the crossbill and black grouse.

The fifth bird on the list was condemned for the fact that it eats pine buds. It's hard to believe that so short a time ago, this bird was viewed as anything other than a victim: it was the capercaillie.

When he heard the owls at midnight,
Hooting, laughing in the forest,
'What is that?' he cried, in terror;
'What is that?' he said, 'Nokomis?'
And the good Nokomis answered:
'That is but the owl and owlet,
Talking in their native language,
Talking, scolding at each other.'

Then the little Hiawatha
Learned of every bird its language,
Learned their names and all their secrets
How they built their nests in summer,
Where they hid themselves in winter,
Talked with them whene'er he met them,
Called them 'Hiawatha's Chickens.'

Henry Wadsworth Longfellow,
The Song of Hiawatha, 1855

PAPERBACK WRITER

What do a scarecrow and a seabird have in common? The answer
lies in the publishing industry: *Worzel Gummidge*, by Barbara
Euphan Todd, was the first book launched in the fledgling Puffin
Story Book series back in 1941. Although the imprint, part of
Penguin Books, had produced a few picture books the previous
year, the tale of the talking scarecrow was the first piece of fiction
from the now well-established label.

AS LAZY AS AN IBIS

In September 2003, a flock of northern bald ibis in Austria discovered a
novel way of making their way to their Italian winter quarters. They
cadged a lift.

The species is being bred at the Konrad Lorenz research centre in
Gruenau, in an attempt to reintroduce it to Austria. Once common, ibis-
es became extinct in the region in the Middle Ages. As a result, they've
got no idea that they should set off for Italy as the weather begins to
turn, so they get driven there. As they get older, they'll be encouraged
along their route by men in hang-gliders, and if the experiment works,
the northern bald ibis will once again be seen in its old European habitat, powering and navigating itself on its twice-yearly 20-day journey.

But for now, they get to sit back and let their private chauffeur take
the strain.

Average incubation time, in days, of the Australian pelican 33

STRANGER AND STRANGER IN PARADISE

Even Linnaeus, that great Swedish taxonomist who took over where Adam left off and named most of the creatures that he knew, made mistakes. One of his best howlers was in naming the greater bird of paradise: he called it *Paradisea apoda*. *Paradisea* makes sense, but *apoda*? That means 'footless'.

Yet Linnaeus can be exonerated. The New Guinea birds were first discovered by westerners in 1512 when Portuguese diplomat Toma Pires visited the Aru islands and was given dead birds of paradise as trade. The islanders told him that they never saw the birds alive, and just found them where they fell from heaven, or paradise. Pires assumed, as did several explorers after him, that the birds fell as they were given to him – the only problem was that the islanders had already cut the feet off to enhance, as they saw it, the singular beauty of the birds.

It was not until the early 19th century that western scientists first discovered that greater birds of paradise, just like every other bird in the world, did in fact have feet. Rather big ones, as it turned out.

NATIONAL BIRDS OF EUROPE

Austria: Barn swallow
Belgium: Kestrel
Denmark: Mute swan
Finland: Whooper swan
France: Unofficially, the rooster
Hungary: Great bustard
Iceland: Gyrfalcon
Luxembourg: Goldcrest
Norway: Dipper
Sweden: Blackbird

IT TAKES TWO

Research conducted by the University of East Anglia in 2004 has confirmed that some migratory birds whose genders winter apart, generally tend to synchronise their arrival upon their return to their breeding grounds. This is an extraordinary feat in the case of the black-tailed godwits monitored in the study: the males and females winter an average 600 miles apart, yet manage to return to their Icelandic breeding grounds simultaneously.

It appears that lateness is not tolerated. During the survey, a few of the males got held up, and returned a day or so late. At least two of them found that their partner had already found a new mate.

The fantastical appearance of the hoopoe (*Upupa epops*) has guaranteed its place in myth and legend, though its significance has varied widely across cultures, continents and centuries.

It has been a symbol of caring for elderly parents and of gratitude in Egyptian hieroglyphs and Christian bestiary writing. It has been a trustworthy and reliable guardian in Jewish mythology, entrusted to protect the shamir worm that helped build Solomon's temple. For later North Africans, it was 'the Doctor', so-called because of the curative and aphrodisiac properties believed to be found in its heart and head.

The hoopoe is also found in Greek mythology, in the story of Philomena and Procne. After these sisters and the latter's husband, Tereus, have committed infidelity, cut out tongues, murdered and dined on sons, and otherwise behaved in ways befitting Greek mythology characters, Philomena is turned into a nightingale, Procne a swallow (or vice versa in different versions of the myth); and Tereus becomes a hoopoe, destined to sing 'poe poe' – 'where where', in Greek – for all eternity as he calls for his lost wife.

The hoopoe has also commonly been thought of as a seer or messenger of wisdom. According to Islamic, Jewish and Christian writings, it was in these capacities that the hoopoe worked to support Solomon's taming of the spirited Queen of Sheba. And in his poetic masterpiece, *The Conference of the Birds*, the twelfth-century poet and saint Farid ud-Din Attar cast the hoopoe as the spiritual leader of all other birds.

In fact, while the moniker hoopoe, like upupa and hud-hud (its Arabic name), is an imitation of the hoopoe's call, its species name derives from the Greek *opopa*, a variant of *horan*, meaning 'to see', and its Hebrew name, *dukhiphat*, is formed from words meaning 'spirit' and 'revelation'. Even the name 'Tereus' comes from the Greek tereo: 'I observe'.

Not everyone, however, has bowed to the wisdom of the hoopoe. An alternative bestiary tale claims that the hoopoe is a signifier not of gratitude or guardianship, but of wicked sinners. Likewise, Leviticus warned that the hoopoe was unclean and its flesh unfit for human consumption. In other quarters the poor hoopoe's expression has been thought so stupid that a bastardisation of its name has come to mean 'to deceive' – to dupe.

But in the face of this hostility, the hoopoe can take comfort that a strict warning has been issued against its harm (again in a medieval Cambridge bestiary): should 'anybody smear himself with the blood of this bird on his way to bed, he will have nightmares about suffocating devils'. Readers may wish to make alternative evening plans accordingly.

And what he saw that morning, he never saw again. He was moved in particular by the children going to school, the silvery-grey pigeons that flew down from the roof to the pavement, and the little loaves of bread, powdered with flour, that some invisible hand had put outside a baker's shop. Those loaves, the pigeons, and the two little boys seemed not of this earth. It all happened at the same time: one of the boys ran towards a pigeon and looked smilingly up at Levin; the pigeon fluttered its wings and flew off, flashing in the sun amid the quivering snow-dust in the air, while from a little window came the smell of fresh-baked bread, and the loaves were put out. All this together was so extraordinarily nice that Levin laughed and cried with delight.

Leo Tolstoy, *Anna Karenina*, 1876

THE LONG AND THE SHORT OF IT

- The bird with the longest scientific name (not including subspecies) is the crowned slaty flycatcher of Latin America: *Griseotyrannus aurantioatrocristatus* (35 letters).
- The bird with the longest scientific name in Europe is the hawfinch: *Coccothraustes coccothraustes* (28 letters).
- Several birds vie for the shortest scientific names with just eight letters, including the corncrake (*Crex crex*) and the magpie (*Pica pica*).
- Incidentally, the longest scientific name in all of nature is that of an amphipod, *Gammaracanthuskytodermogammarus loricatobaicalensis* (50 letters). The shortest is only four letters long, and belongs to a bat: *Ia io*.

BORN TO LOVE BIRDS

One of the most remarkable series of books ever published was finally completed in 2004, 21 years after it first began. The full set of seven volumes of *The Birds of Africa* covers the avifauna of the entire continent, family by family, and is likely never to be surpassed for its clarity, beautiful colour paintings, and authoritative text. Edited by Brown, Fry, Keith and Urban, the full set will set you back around a thousand pounds, particularly as two of the early volumes are now out of print!

But it is for the colour plates that this remarkable series is mentioned here. With the exception of a few illustrations by Peter Hayman in volume I, the entire colour illustration work was handled by one Martin Woodcock... whose namesake, incidentally, appears in volume II.

+ *grain*

Name the flavour
Answer on page 153

QUOTE UNQUOTE

I once had a sparrow alight upon my shoulder for a moment,
while I was hoeing in a village garden, and I felt that I was
more distinguished by that circumstance than I should have
been by any epaulet I could have worn.
HD Thoreau, naturalist and writer

FEED THE BIRDS, CHEAPLY

Clean out an old plastic two-pint milk bottle, and draw a line half
an inch from the bottom along the side opposite the handle. Cut
along this line, and then cut up a further inch. Fold the plastic flap
back inside the bottle. Cut a couple of holes beneath the hole you
have created, and stick two twigs into them. Fill the bottle with
seeds, and hang in the garden. The flap inside the bottle will help
filter the seeds onto the bottom of the bottle, turning it into a
feeding tray.

PIGEON TOWED

A French racing pigeon got badly lost in 2003 when, while heading for Calais, it ended up across the Channel in Warwickshire. No lack of orientation skills here, though... it had got stuck in the radiator grille of a British couple's car.

The bird had hit the car sometime during the couple's weekend break in France, and been carried around on their trip, before being ferried to England at the holiday's close. Only on getting back did the owner notice tufts of feathers sticking out of the front of his vehicle. The bird, named Pierre, was freed, and reunited with his anxious owner.

THE DECLINE OF THE WORLD'S WATERFOWL

Endangered	Swan goose
	White-winged duck
	Hawaiian duck
	Meller's duck
	Madagascar teal
	Brown teal
	White-headed duck
	Blue duck
Critically endangered	Crested shelduck
	Campbell Island teal
	Pink-headed duck
	Madagascar pochard
	Brazilian merganser
Extinct since 1600	Mauritian shelduck
	Mauritian duck
	Amsterdam island duck
	Labrador duck
	Auckland Islands merganser

WHAT'S IN A NAME?

The fulmar, that stiff-winged, winter-hued glider of rocky coastlines, owes its name not to its appearance, but its defence mechanism. Fulmars generate an oily liquid inside their stomachs which they can spit at anyone who comes too close to the nest. The oil is very sticky, and pungent with the odour of fish, giving the bird the Icelandic name ful marr, or 'smelly gull'.

Incidentally, the bird's own olfactory senses, enhanced by its tubular nasal protuberances, are remarkable. It can smell fish oil from up to 15 miles away.

THE GREATEST ENGLISH FOOTBALLERS
THAT EVER FLEW DOWN THE WING

Bobby Moorhen
Jimmy Grebes
Gary Linneter
Hobby Charlton
Nigel Chough
Dion Dunlin
Rodney Marsh Harrier
Peter Osprey
Tom Finchey
Phil Teal
Colin Bellbird

(Please note: Tony Woodcock, Frank Swift and Alvin Martin do not count as they were not real people.)

WINGED WORDS

A starling is on the chimney-top; yonder on the ash tree are four or five of his acquaintance. Suddenly he begins to pour forth a flood of eloquence – facing them as he speaks: Will they come with him down to the field where the cows are grazing? There will be sure to be plenty of insects settling on the grass round the cows, and every now and then they tear up the herbage by the roots and expose creeping things. 'Come', you may hear him say, modulating his tones to persuasion, 'come quickly; you see it is a fresh piece of grass into which the cows have been turned only a few hours since; it was too long for us before, but where they have eaten we can get at the ground comfortably. The water-wagtail is there already; he always accompanies the herd, and will have the pick and choice of everything. Or what do you say to the meadow by the brook? The mowers have begun, and the swathe has fallen before their scythes; there are acres of ground there which we could not touch for weeks; now it is open, and the place is teeming with good food. The finches are there, as busy as may be between the swathes – chaffinch and greenfinch, hedge-sparrow, thrushes, and blackbirds too. Are you afraid? Why, no one shoots in the middle of a summer's day. Still irresolute? (with an angry shrillness). Will you or will you not? (a sharp, short whistle of interrogation). You are simply idiots (finishing with a scream of abuse). I'm off!'

Richard Jefferies,
Wild Life in a Southern County, 1879

DUCK!

Way back in 1437, as workmen were laying the foundations of All Souls College, Oxford, they came across an ancient drain and, piqued by curiosity, peered in. An almighty mallard lay within, and with a few beats of its enormous wings, brushed the workmen aside and flew off as they fell back and gawped. Once they'd pulled themselves together, they set out to find the great beast, but it was never seen again.

For many years afterwards, on every January 14th, the fellows of the college would commemorate the legend by 'Hunting the Mallard', a custom which required white staves, medals and lanterns. It also involved raucous renditions of the Mallard Song throughout the night:

> *Then lett us drink and dance a galliard*
> *in ye remembrance of ye mallard,*
> *And as ye mallard doth in poole,*
> *Lett's dabble, dive and duck in boule.*

In short, Hunting the Mallard, like all good university traditions, was just an excuse for getting completely off your face. Perhaps mindful of the sensibilities of the rest of the good folk of Oxford, the ceremony is now only held once a century, the last occasion being in 2001.

PARTS OF A BIRD'S ANATOMY
YOU REALLY SHOULD KNOW

Maxillary rhamphotheca	Horny sheath on the beak
Operculum	Small ridge inside parrot's nostril
Infundibular cleft	Opening to middle ear from back of throat
Pygostyle	End bone of the spinal column, sometimes called Pope's nose
Propatagium	Fold of skin on wing's leading edge
Hallux	Leading toe

PHONETICALLY SPEAKING

How the Collins Bird Guide *(CBG),* Bill Oddie's Birds of Britain and Ireland, *(BOB),* RSPB Handbook of British Birds *(HBB) and* Observer's Book of Birds *(OBB) hear the waders.*

Golden plover: puu (CBG); floo ee (BOB); pu we (HBB); too-ee (OBB)

Avocet: klup (CBG); kleep (BOB); clute (HBB); kloo-it (OBB)

Green sandpiper: tlueet (CBG); tweet (BOB); tweet (HBB); klee-weet (OBB)

Sanderling: plit (CBG); pip (BOB); twick (HBB); whit (OBB)

QUOTE UNQUOTE

*I value my garden more for being full of blackbirds than of cherries,
and very frankly give them fruit for their songs.*
Joseph Addison, in *The Spectator*, 1712

WHAT'S THE WORZEL THAT CAN HAPPEN?

If you're suddenly transported to a field somewhere in the world, and
you've got no idea which country you're in, ask a scarecrow. If it's
wearing a smile, odds are you're in America, but if it's made out of
animal bones and is brightly coloured, you can narrow your position
down as the south-west of that country. Alternatively, if it frowns at
you you're probably in France. Meanwhile, rice cakes at its feet, and
the costume of the harvest god Sohodo-no-kami on its back will give
your location away as Japan.

Of course, if it talks to you and dances a little jig, you're probably
somewhere near Oz.

BIRDBRAINERS

Penny Casanova. Which bird am I?
Answer on page 153

WAXING LYRICAL

The spoonbill is named for its spatulate bill that aids its feeding techniques, and the goldcrest for the blaze of colour on its head that it uses for display. The waxwing, however, is so-called because of the waxy red tips to its secondary feathers that... er, well they... er...

The jury is still out on that one. Absent in juveniles, the secreted crimson droplets increase as the bird gets older, leading to the likelihood that they are depositories for the indigestible coating of berry fruits that make up much of the bird's diet. It has even been shown that different diets can result in subtly different wing-tip colours. But other birds eat berries, and don't show the results proudly on their feathers. Perhaps the phenomenon is a sign of maturity, experience and success. 'See my bright wing-tips? That means I know where the best berries are. Wanna hang with me?'

Other theories carry less weight. It was once believed in parts of northern America that the red tips proved that the bird was a carnivore, and held its prey steady with its wings, resulting in the tell-tale bloodstains.

The five species categories as defined by the BOU (British Ornithologists' Union):

A. Species which have been recorded in an apparently natural state at least once since 1 January 1950.

B. Species which were recorded in an apparently natural state at least once up to 31 December 1949, but have not been recorded subsequently.

C. Species that, although originally introduced by man, either deliberately or accidentally, have established breeding populations derived from introduced stock, that maintain themselves without necessary recourse to further introduction.

   C1 Naturalised introductions: species that have occurred only as a result of introduction.

   C2 Naturalised establishments: species with established populations as a result of introduction by Man, but which also occur in an apparently natural state.

   C3 Naturalised re-establishments: species with populations successfully re-established by Man in areas of former occurrence.

   C4 Naturalised feral species: domesticated species with populations established in the wild.

   C5 Vagrant naturalised species: species from established naturalised populations abroad.

D. Species that would otherwise appear in Categories A or B except that there is reasonable doubt that they have ever occurred in a natural state. They do not form any part of the species totals, and are not regarded as members of the British List.

E. Species that have been recorded as introductions, transportees or escapees from captivity, and whose breeding populations (if any) are thought not to be self sustaining. Category E species form no part of the British List.

HIGHEST, STRONGEST... SLOWEST

The 2004 Olympics broke several records in the pool and on the track, but it created a new and unwanted one in the air, too. A group of Romanian pigeon-fanciers set free 850 birds in Athens during the games, but only 50 made it back to their homeland, an all-time low for races of this sort.

The blame is being laid squarely at the feet of the media. It appears that the mighty concentration of satellite TV coverage of the Olympics may have interfered with the birds' navigation systems. At least it wasn't steroid abuse.

Most people are familiar with the self-resurrecting phoenix of Egypt, but few in the west have met the Chinese equivalent, Feng Huang. The main difference is that Feng Huang is actually two birds. Feng, the male or yang, represents summer and the solar cycle, while Huang, the female or yin, is the lunar cycle. The continuous cycle of its dual existence gives it eternal life, and means that it does not have to die and be reborn.

Feng Huang tends to appear during times of peace and prosperity, generally when a benign emperor takes the throne. One of the four celestial creatures that created the world (along with the dragon, the unicorn and the tortoise), it holds dominion over the southern, or summer quadrant of the heavens.

If you'd like to see the creature, make your way to the K'unlun mountains of China, where it lives among the wu t'ung trees. Look out for a pheasant-like appearance, with the feathers of a peacock, and a fiery tail emblazoned with the five sacred colours red, blue, yellow, white and black. Alternatively, just sit back and play it a tune. If you're good enough, it will accompany you, and transport you to true bliss.

QUOTE UNQUOTE

If I were reincarnated, I'd want to come back a buzzard. Nothing hates him or envies him or wants him or needs him. He is never bothered or in danger, and he can eat anything.
William Faulkner, novelist

BUMBLING AROUND FOR FOOD

Bee-eaters require about 225 bees, or similar sized insects, to sustain themselves and their young each day. Having caught a bee, the bird carefully rubs it on a perch to squeeze out the venom, and scratch off the insect's poison sacs, before turning it into a meal.

Catching the insect is an even more skilled matter, many species flying below their prey then twisting their heads up to pluck it from the air. Carmine bee-eaters of Africa are possibly the most adventurous of all the family. They follow people and other animals around to pick up on any disturbed insects (a bee-eater riding a stork is a remarkable sight), and hang around near the edge of bushfires to corral what ever tries to flee the flames. They've even been known to catch fish.

But then again, why not? After all, their cousins, the kingfishers, have sometimes been known to catch bees.

A rey zamuro [condor], appearing like a tiny black speck in the blue, stooped, circling prudently with a stealthiness of flight startling in a bird of that great size. The shadow of his pearly-white body, of his black-tipped wings, fell on the grass no more silently than he alighted himself on a hillock of rubbish within three yards of that man, lying as still as a corpse. The bird stretched his bare neck, craned his bald head, loathsome in the brilliance of varied colouring, with an air of voracious anxiety towards the promising stillness of that prostrate body. Then, sinking his head deeply into his soft plumage, he settled himself to wait. The first thing upon which Nostromo's eyes fell on waking was this patient watcher for the signs of death and corruption. When the man got up the vulture hopped away in great, side-long fluttering jumps. He lingered for a while, morose and reluctant, before he rose, circling noiselessly with a sinister droop of beak and claws.

Long after he had vanished, Nostromo, lifting his eyes up to the sky, muttered, 'I am not dead yet'.

Joseph Conrad, Nostromo, 1904

BIRDBRAINERS

Which bird is the noisy 10th of 26?
Answer on page 153

NATURALLY SPEAKING

The long-running *New Naturalist* series from Collins has produced over 90 titles since it began in 1945, but book collectors today pay particularly big money for the monographs that accompanied the series. There were 22 in all, of which 11 were directly about birds:

2.	John Buxton	*The Redstart*
3.	Edward A Armstrong	*The Wren*
4.	Stuart Smith	*The Yellow Wagtail*
5.	Desmond Nethersole-Thompson	*The Greenshank*
6.	James Fisher	*The Fulmar*
9.	Niko Tinbergen	*The Herring Gull's World*
11.	Frank A Lowe	*The Heron*
14.	RC Homes	*Birds of the London Area*
15.	Guy Mountfort	*The Hawfinch*
19.	JD Summers-Smith	*The House Sparrow*
20.	RK Murton	*The Wood Pigeon*

In addition, title number 13 by Miriam Rothschild and Theresa Clay was *Fleas, Flukes and Cuckoos: A Study of Bird Parasites*.

The thunderbird is – almost certainly – a mythical creature, an enormous bird said by the Native Americans, with whose culture it is most strongly associated, to have a wingspan equal to two canoe lengths. With unusual cross-tribal consensus, Native American traditions tell of a bird that made sheets of lightning by winking, lightning bolts by letting forth the glowing snakes it carried with it, and thunder by beating its great wings. Hence it came to be known as the 'thunderbird'. It was not lightning but the bird's razor-sharp claws that ripped the bark off the trees in a storm.

Universally seen as intelligent, powerful and wrathful, there are some variations between tribal mythologies. The Nootka, for example, believed that there was just one Thunderbird, the servant and messenger of the Great Spirit. For the Kwakiutl and Cowichan tribes, thunderbirds were a species, able to take human form by tilting back their beaks and removing their feathers. People were known to have married thunderbirds in their human form, from which unions some still claim ancestry today.

Its image permeates Native American art, crafts and architecture. The thunderbird is a popular crest for totem poles, the Native American equivalent to the European coat-of-arms, and its stylised rendition can be told apart from the raven (another bird of great significance to Native Americans) by its curved beak and outspread wings.

The thunderbird is also seen in other traditions across the world. For example, a northern Asian version of the thunderbird myth says that the bird's immortal heart hangs from a thread in the sky when the bird is dead, and it is the heart's beating that makes the thunder.

But is the thunderbird's existence merely myth? There have been sightings of giant bird-like creatures throughout America, from the 1890s to as recently as 2002, when CNN reported sightings of a bird the size of a small aeroplane around the Alaskan villages of Togiak and Manokotak. And several cryptozoologists have argued that the myth could be founded on genuine sightings, perhaps of a species whose numbers have dwindled in recent centuries but that once flourished in the Native American territories. They suggest that the bird's association with thunder storms might arise from its needing to follow the drafts in order to stay aloft, much as the eagle rides mountain upcurrents.

Fortunately for curious birdwatchers, the thunderbird should be easy to spot: witness accounts suggest a bird similar to the condor, dark in colour, with a 15–20 foot wingspan, and able to lift a deer or human being (as in one case in 1977) from the ground; all in all a bird difficult to confuse with your average garden visitor, the blue tit, dunnock and such-like.

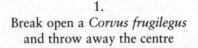

1.
Break open a *Corvus frugilegus*
and throw away the centre

2.
Add one
Phalacrocorax aristotelis

3.
Add

4.
Mix well

Name that bird.
Answer on page 153

QUOTE UNQUOTE

*Marriage is like a cage; one sees the birds outside desperate
to get in, and those inside desperate to get out.*
Montaigne, 16th century French philosopher

Forget your goldcrests and blue tits, chicks and ducklings, the cutest birds in the world are without doubt the tiny todies of the Caribbean. Related to the motmot, there are five species in all (broad-billed, narrow-billed, Cuban, Jamaican and Puerto Rican), and they're cuter than Cutey McCute on his cutest day.

Tame and approachable birds, the todies, which weigh only 0.2oz, are brilliant iridescent green above, with bright red throats and varying pastel colours on their breasts. They spend most of their time just sitting around, suddenly shooting forward to pluck an insect from a nearby leaf. The broad-billed tody, in fact, has never been recorded flying further than 130 feet from one tree to the next. They rarely come down to the ground, either.

This inactivity changes completely during the breeding season, when the birds spend all their time looking for food for their nestlings. In fact, they make up to 140 feeds per chick per day, the highest recorded rate of all birds. Then, once the young leave the nest – actually, a burrow in a bank – it's back to the quiet life, sitting around making barely a sound, and looking – did we mention it? – unbearably cute.

THAT'S ODD

The national bird of Redwing is the turkey.
Er... or maybe that's the other way round.

BORN TO LOVE BIRDS

Jack Gull is probably the less well-known half of the husband and wife team who ran a café in north Norfolk's Cley during the 70s and 80s, which up until its closure in 1988 was the focal point for the nation's twitching communications. The café was named after his wife, Nancy, and is fondly remembered by birders who plied their trade before the fast-link era of pagers and the internet.

Wherever you were in the country, you'd phone in your interesting sightings to Nancy's. In the early days, she'd often record the reports herself, but as the years went on, there was never a shortage of breakfasting birders on hand to jot down the latest rarities. The café was the very hub of information. Planning a trip to the Shetland Isles? Give Nancy's a bell to see if there's anything up there. On holiday in Cornwall? Nancy's will tell you if there's something on your doorstep. The café was THE grapevine, and for about a quid you could settle down with a pot of tea and an Ethelburger (named after the cook) and feel at the centre of the great birdwatching community of Britain.

ABSOLUTELY FABULOUS

The Sick Kite, by Aesop

A kite, sick unto death, said to his mother: 'O Mother! Do not mourn, but at once invoke the gods that my life may be prolonged'. She replied, 'Alas! my son, which of the gods do you think will pity you? Is there one whom you have not outraged by filching from their very altars a part of the sacrifice offered up to them?'

> *We must make friends in prosperity if we*
> *would have their help in adversity.*

WINGED WORDS

There is much of interest and beauty to watch in the ways of birds, and a great pleasure will be added to your country walks if you learn to see them. Cultivate an ear quick to distinguish the different notes and to hear an unknown one among many familiar sounds; and an eye alert to see the least movement among the branches and to notice with one glimpse, enough of the form and colour of a passing bird to recognise it. Birds are difficult to see at first; they will not sit still, like wild flowers, for you to examine them. But how infinitely more interesting and lovable they are, by all the life of them, by the brains and hearts of them!

JA Henderson and MKC Scott, *Birds: Shown series*, 1930s

ONE GOOD TERN

There are four criteria that can qualify a bird as a Red Data species: rarity, localised distribution, declining numbers and international importance. Most birds on the list appear for perhaps one or two of those reasons, but there is one breeding species in Britain that has the misfortune to qualify for all four.

The roseate tern, also recognised as being near threatened with extinction globally, only has about 50 breeding pairs in Britain, although a current BAP (Biodiversity Action Plan) aims to quadruple that figure by 2008.

This is truly a beautiful bird. Its long tail streamers flutter out behind as it appears to ghost along in the winds of the few east coast sites where it still nests. Perhaps it was one of the species that so inspired St Cuthbert, when he made the islands off the Northumbrian coast in the late 7th century his home, in order to devote his time to bird protection. The saint introduced laws protecting eider ducks (known as cuddy ducks) and other nesting seabirds in the Farne Islands – thought to be the earliest recorded bird protection laws in the world.

The bird of paradise alights only upon the hand that does not grasp.
John Berry, musician

NORTHERN IRISH AVIAN PLACE NAMES

Name	Meaning
Drumiller	Hill of the eagles
Craignashoke	Rock of hawks
Tullycoe	Hillock of cuckoos
Kilnahushogue	Lark's wood
Craignagolman	Rock of pigeons
Lisnagelvin	Fort of sparrows
Ruenascarrive	Land of the cormorants
Drumdran	Wrens' ridge
Binnafreaghan	Crows' peak

THE WILLOW WEEPS FOR THEE

The willow pattern has become such a familiar porcelain image that the two birds in the top left-hand corner are as recognisable as almost any other avian image. But what are they doing there; what part do they play in the drama that unfolds in the Chinese scenario below?

Koong-se was the beautiful daughter of a powerful mandarin. His secretary, Chang, had fallen in love with her. Banishing his lowly servant for these romantic ideas above his station, the mandarin built a fence around his estate to keep Koong-se in and Chang out, although Chang kept in contact with his beloved by floating shells down river to her.

One day, the mandarin invited a noble duke to a banquet, with the idea of offering him Koong-se's hand in marriage as dessert. Sneaking into the feast disguised as a servant, Chang found Koong-se and began his dramatic rescue. They were spotted at the last moment, but escaped across a bridge over the river. The mandarin tried hard to get his daughter back, but Chang was always one step ahead, and the couple eventually moved to a distant island where Chang took to the pen and became a famous writer. As so often the case with writers, his new career did for him. The mandarin discovered him through his work, and had him killed, Koong-se killing herself out of grief.

But the tale did not go unnoticed by the gods, who immortalised the young lovers as doves, in which form they fly together to this day in the open freedom of the sky.

Sir Edward Grey, later Viscount Grey of Fallodon, holds the record for the longest continuous term as British Foreign Secretary, hanging on to the job for 11 years. Not bad, until you consider that his term stretched from 1905 to 1916, making him the man on the job when Europe bared its swords and entered a war which led to loss of life on a scale previously unimaginable. 'The lamps are going out,' he muttered dolefully from his window, 'all over Europe.' As Foreign Secretary, perhaps he should have done something about it, but then Edward Grey had more to interest him than just politics.

He was passionate about birds, so much so that in 1927 he penned an adulatory little tome called *The Charm of Birds*, principally about birdsong. 'My opportunities for watching birds have been intermittent,' he wrote with great bathos. 'One who reviews pleasant experiences and puts them on record increases the value of them to himself; he gathers up his own feelings and reflections, and is thereby better able to understand and to measure the fullness of what he has enjoyed.' For a man who had played a part in allowing the Great War to happen, these expressed sentiments would have hidden so much.

Yet Grey's love of birds was recognised by, among others, the great ornithologist and naturalist Max Nicholson, who in 1938, five years after Grey's death, co-founded the Edward Grey Institute of Field Ornithology.

Today, the man is remembered for far more than his politics.

A RING OUZEL BY ANY OTHER NAME

Regional names for *Turdus torquatus*:
Cowboy (Tipperary)
Ditch blackie (East Lothian)
Flitterchack (Orkney)
Michaelmas blackbird (Dorset)
Mountain colley (Somerset)
Whistler (Wicklow)

CASTE LIST

Keeping up Appearances, that 90s sitcom about the importance of apparent status, and in which Bucket is pronounced Bouquet, would appear to be peculiarly British. Not so. The programme has been refilmed for audiences around the world, including India, where the Hindi version is called *The Crow that tried to Walk like a Swan*.

ABSOLUTELY FABULOUS

The Jackdaw and the Doves, by Aesop

A jackdaw, seeing some doves in a cote abundantly provided with food, painted himself white and joined them in order to share their plentiful maintenance. The doves, as long as he was silent, supposed him to be one of themselves and admitted him to their cote. But when one day he forgot himself and began to chatter, they discovered his true character and drove him forth, pecking him with their beaks. Failing to obtain food among the doves, he returned to the jackdaws. They too, not recognising him on account of his colour, expelled him from living with them.

He who tries to belong to both camps, belongs to neither

NATIONAL BIRDS OF THE EAST

Bangladesh: Doel, or magpie robin
Myanmar: Burmese peacock
India: Peacock
Indonesia: Javan hawk eagle
Japan: Kiyi, or green pheasant
Korea: Black-billed magpie
Nepal: Impeyan pheasant
Philippines: Monkey-eating eagle
Sri Lanka: Ceylon jungle fowl
Thailand: Siamese fireback pheasant

WINGED WORDS

Here I am in my valise on the floor of my dugout writing before sleeping. The artillery is like a stormy tide breaking on the shores of the full moon that rides high and clear among white cirrus clouds. It has been a day of cold feet in the OP. I had to go unexpectedly. When I posted my letter and Civil Liabilities paper in the morning I thought it would be a bad day, but we did all the shelling. Hardly anything came near the OP or even the village. I simply watched the shells changing the landscape. The pretty village among trees that I first saw two weeks ago in now just ruins among violated stark tree trunks. But the sun shone and larks and partridge and magpies and hedgesparrows made love and the trench was being made passable for the wounded that will be harvested in a day or two. Either the Bosh is beaten or he is going to surprise us. The air was full of aeroplane fights. I saw one enemy fall on fire and one of ours tumble into the enemy's wire. I am tired but resting.

**Edward Thomas' letter home from Arras to his wife Helen,
7 or 8 April 1917. On 9 April, he was killed by a shell-blast.**

= *Hidden by the beeches*

Name that phrase.
Answer on page 153

QUOTE UNQUOTE

When thou seest an eagle, thou seest a
portion of genius; lift up thy head!
William Blake, poet

FLEEING THE PIGEON-HOLE

Walking down a wooded lane, most of us have experienced the alarming explosion of woodpigeons as they suddenly thrash their way out of nearby branches on our approach. Their panicking struggle to get away suggests they only saw us at the last moment... yet not so. The likelihood is that the bird has been watching us for some time.

As large birds, woodpigeons need a fraction longer than other tree-dwellers to get themselves going, which in a fight or flight world could be their downfall. Hence their trick. They wait until their potential predator is almost upon them, then deliberately clatter their wings as they take off. The effect is startling, giving the bird precious moments to get away.

One day, Tanemahuta, father of the trees, was walking through the forest. He looked up at his children reaching for the sky and he noticed that they were starting to sicken, as insects were eating them at their base. He talked to his brother, Tanehokahoka, who called all of his children, the birds of the air, together. Tanemahuta spoke to them.

'Something is eating my children, the trees. I need one of you to come down from the forest roof and live on the floor, so that my children can be saved, and your home can be saved. Who will come?'

Tanehokahoka turned to Tui. 'Tui, will you come down from the forest roof?'

'No, Tanehokahoka, for it is too dark and I am afraid of the dark.'

Then Tanehokahoka asked Pukeko. 'No, Tanehokahoka, for it is too damp down there and I do not want to get my feet wet.'

Then Tanehokahoka asked Pipiwharauroa. 'No, Tanehokahoka, for I am busy at the moment building my nest.'

So Tanehokahoka turned to Kiwi. Kiwi looked up at the trees and saw the sun filtering through the leaves. Kiwi looked around and saw his family. Kiwi looked at the cold damp earth. Looking around once more, he turned to Tanehokahoka and said: 'I will come down.'

Great was the joy in the hearts of Tanehokahoka and Tanemahuta, for this little bird was giving them hope. But Tanemahuta felt that he should warn Kiwi.

'Kiwi, do you realise that if you do this, you will have to grow thick, strong legs so that you can rip apart the logs on the ground and you will lose your beautiful coloured feathers and wings so that you will never be able to return to the forest roof. You will never see the light of day again.'

Kiwi took one last look at the sun filtering through the trees and said a silent goodbye. Kiwi took one last look at the other birds, their wings and their coloured feathers, and said a silent goodbye. Then he turned to Tanehokahoka and said: 'I will still come down.'

Then Tanehokahoka turned to the other birds and said: 'Tui, because you were too scared to come down from the forest roof, you will wear the two white feathers at your throat as the mark of a coward. Pukeko, because you did not want to get your feet wet, you will live forever in the swamp. Pipiwharauroa, because you were too busy building your nest, you will never build another nest again, but lay your eggs in other birds' nests. But you Kiwi, because of your great sacrifice, you will become the most well known and most loved bird of them all.'

When Brandon Lee, son of martial arts legend Bruce, died during the making of the 90s cult film *The Crow*, two things happened. The shocking nature of his death surely helped the box office and continued success of the film, but it also led to great intrigue and speculation which continues to this day.

Lee played a character called Alex Draven, killed, along with his girlfriend, by a gang of thugs on Hallowe'en. Brought back to life by a crow, he spends the rest of the film gaining bloody revenge on his murderers. As he is now among the undead, knives and bullets can't hurt him, and it was during the filming of one such sequence that Lee was killed, shot by a gun that was supposed to be full of blanks but carried live ammunition.

The inevitable conspiracy theories began. Had Lee learned too much about martial arts truth and Chinese underworld practices, and needed to be offed? Had he stumbled upon a real process for raising the dead? Had he even come so far in his thinking that he loaded the gun himself believing that he would one day return?

Load of nonsense, of course, but it did the film (unlike its star) no harm. Lee's gothic face, accompanied by a crow, has become an iconic symbol of the darker blurring of the real world and that of Hollywood.

CLOSER TO DEATH THAN JAMES BOND

Several species of bird, such as the nene or the Mauritian kestrel, have been brought back from the brink of extinction in recent decades, but none, surely, has come as close to the end as the Laysan duck. Once widespread on Hawaii, its population went into freefall from 1902 once rabbits had been introduced to the islands. The rabbits destroyed the vegetation that was relied upon by the insects that are the bird's main food supply, and by 1911, there were only six or seven of the ducks left.

And then it got worse. In 1930, a survey of the islands revealed that only one female remained. She had at least mated, but the future of the species lay in one small clutch of eggs.

And then it got worse again. The male disappeared, and the eggs were destroyed by a passing curlew. That was it, it was over. Another species lost thanks to the meddling of... but wait! It turned out that the female had enough semen stored in her oviduct to produce one more clutch of eggs. Life! From this last desperate act of death defiance, a new era was born. The rabbit population was eradicated, and the duck numbers began to rise. Today, the Laysan duck is still very endangered in the wild, but is being looked after in captivity until such times as its habitat can be restored, and you can see the descendants of that miraculous little clutch of eggs at several of the WWT's UK centres.

---

54 *Punch-blocking move number in the traditional Kenpo karate system entitled 'Plucking a bird from the sky'*

AN AUKWARD BIRD

The great auk, probably the most famous of the extinct birds after the dodo, breathed its last in 1844. It may have suffered from the want of useful wings, but it certainly didn't suffer from the want of descriptions:

- *Anser magellanicus* – 17th century specific name, from a time when the bird was classed as a goose
- **Anglemager** – a Norwegian name, based on its call ('aangla') that fishermen used as their cue to start getting their hooks ready
- **Garefowl** – Icelandic, meaning 'spear-billed bird'
- **Isarokitosk** – Inuit for 'he who has little wings'
- **Penguin** – 'the fat one', from the Latin 'pinguis' meaning fat; although possibly from 'pin-wing', short for pinioned wing, referring to the bird's inability to fly. The name is now, of course, used by an entirely different family
- **Tossefugl** – Danish, meaning 'stupid bird'
- **Wobble** – a Newfoundland name based on the bird's gait.

BIRDBRAINERS

The name of which occasional British bird
contains four consecutive vowels?
Answer on page 153

LOVE IS IN THE AIR

The association of St Valentine with love stems from Chaucer's poem, *The Parliament of Fowls*, in which the various birds of the air meet up on the saint's feast day and declare their ardour. Yet Valentine's Day is on February 14, well before the usual bird mating season. Was Chaucer some sort of a fool?

No. He wrote the poem in 1381 to commemorate the marriage of Richard II to Anne of Bohemia which took place on May 3. Looking around for a suitable symbolism, he discovered that a relatively obscure saint by the name of Valentine of Genoa celebrated his feast on that day, and his poem could go ahead.

Trouble was, St Valentine's Day already existed. Pope Gelasius I had in 496 taken a mid-February Roman Lupercalian festival celebrating fertility and assigned it to another St Valentine, a Roman priest, fixing the date on February 14, the day of his martyrdom. But by the 15th century, Chaucer's loving Valentine connotations had taken root, and the February date shifted in its emphasis towards the romantic, where it remains to this day. Mercenary pink card and teddy-bear sellers apart, that is.

Metabolic rate, in kJ, per day of a breeding storm petrel. The metabolic rate   55
of a 30-year-old man is about 2000kJ

Birds as observed by Gilbert White in his
Natural History of Selborne, 1788/9

I was much pleased to see, among the collection of birds from Gibraltar, some of those short-winged English summer birds of passage, concerning whose departure we have made so much inquiry. Now if these birds are found in Andalusia to migrate to and from Barbary, it may easily be supposed that those that come to us may migrate back to the continent, and spend their winters in some of the warmer parts of Europe. This is certain, that many soft-billed birds that come to Gibraltar appear there only in spring and autumn, seeming to advance in pairs towards the northward, for the sake of breeding during the summer months; and retiring in parties and broods towards the south at the decline of the year: so that the rock of Gibraltar is the great rendezvous, and place of observation, from whence they take their departure each way towards Europe or Africa. It is therefore no mean discovery, I think, to find that our small short-winged summer birds of passage are to be seen spring and autumn on the very skirts of Europe; it is a presumptive proof of their emigrations.

QUOTE UNQUOTE

People expect the clergy to have the grace of a swan, the friendliness of a sparrow, the strength of an eagle and the night hours of an owl – and some people expect such a bird to live on the food of a canary.
Edward Jeffrey, British clergyman

THE GREATEST ENGLISH CRICKETERS
EVER TO MAKE A DUCK

Graham Goose
Fred Titmouse
Alan Knot
Bill Ostrich
Bruce Finch
Darren Chough
Jim Saker
Wayne Larks
Brian Rosefinch
Mark Butcherbird
Chris Broad-billed Sandpiper

(Please note: Dermot Reeve, Peter Martin and Alfred Dipper do not count as they were not real people.)

Number of species of Hawaiian bird known from fossil records to have become extinct

WHAT'S IN A NAME?

Hungry birds of the sea that look rather like black crows were once understandably given the name *corvus marinus*. In time, this contracted to cormorant, although the species has developed more of an inland distribution in recent times. The cormorant's cousin, the shag, has a similarly straightforward etymology. Settle down at the back, there. It's named from the Old Norse skegg, or beard, which became Old English sceacga, or hair, and was used to describe its crest. Shag pile rugs have the same origin.

BIRDS TO LOOK OUT FOR
WHEN YOU'RE THIRSTY

Milky stork
Cocoa thrush
Cisti cola
Mead-ow pipit
Jameson's antpecker
Stout-billed cuckooshrike
Claret-breasted fruit-dove
Wine-throated hummingbird
Or just put your feet up with a nice cup of tea-l or a pint of bitter-n

WINGED WORDS

For most birders there is only one thing better than seeing good birds. You can probably guess what it is… it's actually finding the thing for yourself. In fact for some people finding rarities is the raison d'être of their birding selves. That act of independent discovery has been elevated almost to the status of a principle, which often forms the basis of opposition to twitching. Some argue that without those who go faithfully to watch the same area day in, day out, in the hope they might find something unusual, no rare birds would ever be discovered. Twitchers, by contrast, are viewed as parasitic upon the endeavours of these other honest ornithological toilers, who are known as 'patch-workers'.

I'm not sure the argument is valid. The fact is that many birders both twitch others' rarities and also work a local patch themselves. After all, the two things are not mutually exclusive. In fact they are in many ways interdependent. Finding rarities is enormously satisfying, but if we're honest a major part of the thrill is the kudos derived from our peers' metaphoric thumbs of approval. Without the rare bird being found there would certainly be no twitch. But then without the twitch there can be no glory or, at least, much less glory.

Mark Cocker, *Birders: Tales of a Tribe*, 2001

Henna tattoo symbols explained

Bird	Birth and fecundity, deep intuition
Crow	Revival
Dove	A blessing for long and perilous travels
Eagle	Might and war, plus spiritual growth
Hawk	Self-discipline
Parrot	The beauty of life and its distant horizons
Raven	Hidden knowledge

QUOTH THE RAVEN: TWENTY-FOUR

Birds are not known for their ability to count – indeed in the bad old egg-collecting days of yore, the common theory was that if you left three eggs in the nest, the adults wouldn't notice that some had gone. This mathematical wobbliness has also helped photographers obtain close-ups of birds on the nest, back in the days before zoom photography had really kicked in. Construct your hide near the nest, and then walk into it with an assistant. The adult, keeping its distance, will be watching. When your assistant casually wanders out again, the bird will think the hide empty, and return to the nest.

As photographer Eric Hosking discovered in 1937, however, the process wasn't so easy with ravens. Among the most intelligent of birds, ravens can count. Two go in, one comes out, one must be left. They wouldn't come back to the nest. The only way that Hosking was able to get his shots was to baffle the birds with high numbers. So he took a party of schoolchildren into the hide, and when they left en masse, with Hosking still inside, the birds decided the coast was clear, and came back to be immortalised in Hosking's photography.

BIRDS OF THE NIGHT

Avian constellations include:

Apus, the Bird of Paradise......................Found in the southern skies
Aquila, the Eagle ....The bird is carrying a small boy
Columba, the Dove ....It is carrying an olive branch
Corvus, the Crow ....Contains five stars
Grus, the Crane..Formerly part of Pisces
Pavo, the Peacock ....The constellation represents the tail
Phoenix..Formerly known as The Boat
Tucana, the Toucan ....With Pavo and Apus, grouped
around the South Pole
...and The Big Dipper..Part of Ursa Major

On the 29th of April, as I was fishing from the bank of the river near the Nine-Acre-Corner bridge, standing on the quaking grass and willow roots, where the muskrats lurk, I heard a singular rattling sound, somewhat like that of the sticks which boys play with their fingers, when, looking up, I observed a very slight and graceful hawk, like a nighthawk, alternately soaring like a ripple and tumbling a rod or two over and over, showing the under side of its wings, which gleamed like a satin ribbon in the sun, or like the pearly inside of a shell. This sight reminded me of falconry and what nobleness and poetry are associated with that sport. The merlin it seemed to me it might be called; but I care not for its name. It was the most ethereal flight I had ever witnessed. It did not simply flutter like a butterfly, nor soar like the larger hawks, but it sported with proud reliance in the fields of air; mounting again and again with its strange chuckle, it repeated its free and beautiful fall, turning over and over like a kite, and then recovering from its lofty tumbling, as if it had never set its foot on terra firma. It appeared to have no companion in the universe – sporting there alone – and to need none but the morning and the ether with which it played. It was not lonely, but made all the earth lonely beneath it.

HD Thoreau, *Walden*, 1854

BIRDBRAINERS

What am I?
RID   GE
Answer on page 153

BORN TO LOVE BIRDS

There's rather a sweet irony that one of the main ornithological reference tomes of recent years, *The Birdwatcher's Dictionary*, was written by a man who could have been an entry himself. Peter Weaver, who was born in 1944, published the book in 1981 and it soon gained authoritative status. Full of interesting definitions such as 'Watching Back: Locating a nest by disturbing its owner, waiting for the bird to return and noting exactly where it goes. This technique is useful where nests are hidden in thick cover', and 'Peep: One of the smaller members of the genus *Calidris*, part of the family *Scolopacidae*. Examples of peeps are the Little Stint and the Dunlin', its contents are now available on the internet.

Although his name might suggest a fondness for sparrows, Weaver's main interest lies in seabirds, in particular the fulmar.

BIRD BOSSES

Golden monarch
Emperor penguin
King eider
Imperial shag
Queen whydah
Timalia pileata dictator, a subspecies of the chestnut-capped babbler
Little ground tyrant

And the most ironfisted of them all:
Tyrannus melancholicus despotes,
a subspecies of the tropical kingbird

BRITONS PINCH A MARTIN

When a purple martin turned up at the lighthouse on the extreme northwest corner of the Butt of Lewis in September 2004, Britain's twitchers dropped everything in an attempt to get up there and see it. The bird was not only a first for Britain, but for Europe to boot, having crossed the Atlantic from its usual home. As the bird is migratory, leaving its breeding grounds in North America in late summer to winter in South America, this one individual must have been blown by the season's hurricanes off course. Way off course.

Great though the British fervour was, it was nothing compared to the love shown the martin by householders up and down the eastern seaboard of the US. Ever since native Americans started centuries ago to put gourds up for the birds to nest in, the purple martin in the east of the country has entirely abandoned its practice of finding old woodpecker tree cavities, and relies heavily on man-made and man-offered homes.

Should people lose interest in looking after the bird's needs, it would be in trouble, but fortunately there's no sign of that happening. Whole organisations are set up to encourage and advise 'landlords' on best living arrangements for the hirundine, while purple-martin events are regularly and enthusiastically attended. Products to fuel the interest are multifarious, from plastic gourds (would you prefer the Natureline model or Troyer Horizontal, or perhaps you'd like to invest in a deluxe rack system?) to nest-checking tools and sanctuary signs. The Purple Martin Conservation Association has a website dispensing advice on how to modify martin houses, best martin management tips, and helpful hints for landlords.

It's estimated that there are up to one million people who, with varying degrees of success, look after the purple martin each year.

It's a gander magic
Queen

HAMMERED INTO SUBMISSION

The crow is a well-known harbinger of bad luck in Britain, but in South Africa it's a different bird that strikes nervous tension into the hearts of the superstitious: the hamerkop. This curious bird, distantly related to herons and storks, is a symbol of vanity and futility, probably because as it stands quietly fishing in a stream, it appears to be admiring its own reflection. The sight of a hamerkop feather floating down a river is said to represent the temporary quality of human life, drifting away into history.

The bird is believed to bring disaster, too, and children sing songs encouraging it to leave. If one flies above a village, a death will occur, and to dream of the hamerkop means, quite frankly, you've had it.

Number, in thousands, of oiled seabirds picked up after the Erika *sinking off* 61
the Brittany coast in 1999

YOU CAN'T HAVE A BIRD BOOK
WITHOUT PARROT JOKES

A woman is walking down the street to work and sees a parrot in a pet shop. She stops to look at the bird, which stares at her squarely in the eye and says: 'Hey lady, you really are ugly.' The woman is shocked, and storms off to work in a foul mood. The next day she's walking past again, and she throws a glance at the parrot, which tips its head and says back: 'Hey lady, you really are ugly.'

Now she's really livid, so she storms into the pet shop and marches straight up to the owner.

'Listen', she demands, 'if that parrot calls me ugly once more, I'll sue you to high heaven and back again, and have the bird killed into the bargain. Well?'

The owner apologises profusely and promises it will never happen again.

The next day she's walking past the pet shop and she slows down. She stops, and faces the parrot, narrowing her eyes and waiting. 'Hey lady,' says the bird.

She leans forward towards him, clenching her fists and waiting. 'Yessss', she says slowly. The bird shuffles back and forth on its perch. Many seconds pass. Finally, the parrot opens its beak.

'You know.'

QUOTE UNQUOTE

The moment a little boy is concerned with which is a jay and which is a sparrow, he can no longer see the birds or hear them sing.
Eric Berne, social psychologist

FAECAL POINT

Recent evidence has shed intriguing light on one of the bird world's more unusual habits. The burrowing owls of America collect mammal droppings which they scatter in and around their holes, a behaviour long believed to be an attempt to disguise their own scent from potential predators. But new research suggests that the droppings are not so much used as a repellent, but as a lure for one of their favourite meals: the dung beetle.

The researchers, who analysed the pellets of the owls, found that the birds from droppings-adorned burrows got through 10 times as many dung beetles as those whose burrows had been cleared of droppings.

Not so much horses for courses as faeces for species.

Alabama	*Yellowhammer*
Alaska	*Willow ptarmigan*
Arizona	*Cactus wren*
Arkansas	*Mockingbird*
California	*California valley quail*
Colorado	*Lark bunting*
Connecticut	*Robin*
Delaware	*Blue hen chicken*
Florida	*Mockingbird*
Georgia	*Brown thrasher*
Hawaii	*Nene*
Idaho	*Mountain bluebird*
Illinois	*Cardinal*
Indiana	*Cardinal*
Iowa	*Eastern goldfinch*
Kansas	*Western meadowlark*
Kentucky	*Cardinal*
Louisiana	*Eastern brown pelican*
Maine	*Chickadee*
Maryland	*Baltimore oriole*
Massachusetts	*Chickadee*
Michigan	*Robin*
Minnesota	*Common loon*
Mississippi	*Mockingbird*
Missouri	*Bluebird*
Montana	*Western meadowlark*
Nebraska	*Western meadowlark*
Nevada	*Mountain bluebird*
New Hampshire	*Purple finch*
New Jersey	*Eastern goldfinch*
New Mexico	*Roadrunner*
New York	*Bluebird*
North Carolina	*Cardinal*
North Dakota	*Western meadowlark*
Ohio	*Cardinal*
Oklahoma	*Scissor-tailed flycatcher*
Oregon	*Western meadowlark*
Pennsylvania	*Ruffed grouse*
Rhode Island	*Rhode Island red*
South Carolina	*Great Carolina wren*
South Dakota	*Ring-necked pheasant*
Tennessee	*Mockingbird*
Texas	*Mockingbird*
Utah	*California seagull*
Vermont	*Hermit thrush*
Virginia	*Cardinal*
Washington	*Willow goldfinch*
West Virginia	*Cardinal*
Wisconsin	*Robin*
Wyoming	*Western meadowlark*

CROSSED LINES

It's ironic that Britain's only endemic species, found nowhere else in the world, is also one of the hardest to identify. Scotland's crossbills have always been difficult to pick apart, the common version being slightly smaller than the occasional parrot crossbills that come in from Scandinavia, but in recent years the situation has become more complicated. A third species was identified as being of intermediate size between the two, and the Scottish crossbill gained specific status of its own.

The trouble is, it's so difficult to identify in the field. A relic of the ancient Caledonian pine forests of the central and eastern Highlands, it has a slightly heavier bill than the common variety, but individuals vary. It's thought there are around a thousand pairs of the bird – making this the entire world population.

Many theories, even phrenological theories, have been advanced to explain the origin of the cuckoo laying its eggs in other birds' nests. M. Prevost [a French scientist] alone, I think, has thrown light by his observations on this puzzle: he finds that the female cuckoo, which, according to most observers, lays at least from four to six eggs, must pair with the male each time after laying only one or two eggs. Now, if the cuckoo was obliged to sit on her own eggs, she would either have to sit on all together, and therefore leave those first laid so long, that they probably would become addled; or she would have to hatch separately each egg, or two eggs, as soon as laid: but as the cuckoo stays a shorter time in this country than any other migratory bird, she certainly would not have time enough for the successive hatchings. Hence we can perceive in the fact of the cuckoo pairing several times, and laying her eggs at intervals, the cause of her depositing her eggs in other birds' nests, and leaving them to the care of foster-parents. I am strongly inclined to believe that this view is correct, from having been independently led to an analogous conclusion with regard to the South American ostrich, the females of which are parasitical, if I may so express it, on each other; each female laying several eggs in the nests of several other females, and the male ostrich undertaking all the cares of incubation, like the strange foster-parents with the cuckoo.

Charles Darwin,
The Voyage of the Beagle, 1839

THE ANCIENT TIMES OF NURSERY RHYMES

Who was Mother Goose, anyway? Back in medieval France, the village geese were often left in the hands of one of the elderly women of the village. Such women gained a reputation for whiling away their time by telling stories, so when Charles Perrault anthologised eight legendary tales in 1697, he subtitled his collection 'Contes de ma Mère l'Oye'. This title was translated by Robert Samber in 1729 as 'Tales of Mother Goose', and the old woman had entered the story-telling canon.

However, some researchers believe that Mother Goose had a more legendary status, a sort of fairy birdmother who calmed children with her tales. She is believed to have taken shape from the 8th century noblewoman Bertrada of Laon, whose son Charlemagne (Charles the Great) founded the Holy Roman Empire. While Charlemagne was young, Bertrada educated him, and earned a reputation as a patroness of children. She was sometimes known as Bertha Greatfoot, or, because of the size of the birds' appendages, Queen Goosefoot.

QUOTE UNQUOTE

If I had to choose, I would rather have birds than airplanes.
Charles Lindbergh, early aviator

THE PC VIEW OF WILDFOWL

British ducks and geese run through a spellchecker:

Anas clypeata (Shoveler) becomes Anal clipart
Anser fabalis (Bean goose) becomes Answer fabulist
Aythya fuligula (Tufted duck) becomes Althea follicular
Branta leucopsis (Barnacle goose) becomes Brenda leucosis
Mergellus albellus (Smew) becomes Marcellus labellers
Somateria spectabilis (Eider) becomes Nonmaterial spectacles

THE MILK OF AVIAN KINDNESS

When is a bird like a mammal? When it's a pigeon, flamingo or emperor penguin. Not funny? Not meant to be. These three birds actually feed milk to their young, and each for different reasons.

The pigeon's offering to its squabs, known as crop milk, is formed from the liquid-filled lining of its crop. It's more nutritious than cow's milk, and provides the nestlings with the protein that most other young get from insects. It enables the young to grow rapidly the body fat that characterises the bird.

For the young flamingo, as its specially adapted filtering bill develops, liquid would be hard to take on board, so for the first two months of its life, its parent feeds it with fatty milk that is generated by glands inside the digestive tract.

The young emperor penguin's needs are completely different: the treacherous Antarctic terrain may mean that its mother, off foraging for food while the father incubates the egg, might not return in time for the hatching. The father is therefore able to feed its young for a few days with milk formed within its oesophagus, until the mother returns.

Bird milk is also available to humans. It's the name of a Russian chocolate... made from cocoa, though, not stomach lining.

IN TROUBLE WITH THE BILL

Doing a bit of bird? The word comes from the ever dependable rhyming slang of those born with Bow Bells ringing in their ears. Birdlime equals time.

The number of times the following bird words occur in the works of Shakespeare, not including plurals or compounds. For one more, see page 52.

Fly	251
Swift	77
Crow	34
Eagle	29
Owl	26
Robin	25
Fowl	15
Duck	11
Gull	11
Sparrow	11
Hawk	8
Birding	5
Bill	16
Oddie	0

QUOTE UNQUOTE

The swallows are flocking together in the skies ready for departing and a crowd has dropt to rest on the walnut tree where they twitter as if they were telling their young stories of their long journey to cheer and check fears.
John Clare, poet

CORMOREAGLE

Two of them, each 18 feet tall, tower over the streets of Liverpool; they sit on the crests of Anfield's famous football club; but what exactly are the Liver Birds?

In 1207 King John realised that Liverpool (Lerpole as it was then known) was a perfect port and stronghold as he tried to establish a military strength against Wales and Ireland. Granting the site a 'charter of liberties', he gave the city's leaders the right to use in their seal his own symbol, the Plantagenet emblem of a black eagle with a sprig of broom in its beak. Centuries passed, and when Cavalier forces took Liverpool in 1644, the official seal was destroyed. Eleven years later it was replaced by a new one... with a few differences. The bird held the same pose as the eagle, but had become considerably more svelte, resembling the cormorants – or 'laver' (seaweed) birds – that crowded the city's docks. The hybrid was born.

A caged bird in spring knows quite well that he might serve some end; he feels well enough that there is something for him to do, but he cannot do it. What is it? He does not remember too well. Then he has some vague ideas and says to himself: 'The others make their nests and lay their eggs and bring up their little ones,' and so he knocks his head against the bars of the cage. But the cage remains and the bird is maddened by anguish.

'Look at the lazy animal,' says another bird that passes by, 'he seems to be living at his ease.' Yes, the prisoner lives, he does not die, there are no outward signs of what passes within him; his health is good, he is more or less gay when the sun shines. But then comes the season of migration, bringing attacks of melancholia. 'But he has got everything he wants,' say the children that tend him in his cage, while he looks through the bars at the overcast sky, where a thunderstorm is gathering, and he inwardly rebels against his fate. 'I am caged, I am caged, and you tell me I do not want anything, fools! You think I have everything I need! Oh! I beseech you, liberty, so that I can be a bird like other birds!'

...Men are often prevented by circumstances from doing things, imprisoned in I do not know what horrible, horrible, most horrible cage. There is also, I know it, the deliverance, the tardy deliverance. A just or unjustly ruined reputation, poverty, inevitable circumstances, adversity, that is what makes men prisoners.

Vincent van Gogh, *from his letters to his brother Theo, July 1880*

BIRDS YOU MIGHT MYTH

If you want to know the answer to anything, absolutely anything, forget Google. Go and ask the Simurgh. It has been around for so long that it has even seen the world destroyed three times, and its mighty longevity has enabled it to absorb all knowledge and understanding.

Unsurprisingly, this wise Persian bird once lived in the Tree of Knowledge, whose branches contain the seeds of every plant that ever existed. Don't go looking for it there, though: it left many moons ago (and in taking flight, shook the seeds from the Tree and scattered them across the world) and now lives on the sacred mountain of Alburz, which no-one has ever been able to climb.

If you've been in the wars, however, it might be worth trying the ascent. This giant monster is able to heal the most terrible of wounds with but a single touch.

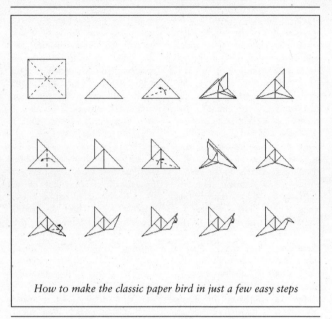

How to make the classic paper bird in just a few easy steps

EVERYONE HATES BIRD SONG

In 2000, an internet music site, dotmusic, commissioned a poll to discover the most irritating pop song ever created (the term 'created' being used very loosely here). The top ten included several obvious musical criminals, from Black Lace to the Teletubbies, St Winifred's School Choir to Chris de Burgh, but perched on the highest twig was the 1981 cringe-fest that became the staple self-humiliation of package holiday-makers throughout the next decade: The Birdie Song.

The lyricless, arm-flapping, lah-lah-lahing number was actually first written in the 1950s by Swiss accordion player and wildfowl tender Werner Thomas, who initially called it The Duck's Dance. No-one paid much attention. In 1963, aged 71, while providing the live music in a German club, he decided to give the ditty another go, and found that everybody was dancing to it. The craze caught on.

Since then, there have been over 140 versions of the tune worldwide, from Australia to the US, and about 40 million copies sold. When the Tweets launched it in the early 1980s, the British, too, became infected, and European island life during the holiday season has never been the same.

NATIONAL BIRDS OF CENTRAL AMERICA AND THE CARIBBEAN

Anguilla: Mourning dove
Bahamas: Greater flamingo
Belize: Keel-billed toucan
Bermuda: White-tailed tropicbird
Cuba: Clay-coloured robin
Dominican Republic: Palm-chat
Grenada: Grenada dove
Guatemala: Quetzal
Guyana: Canje pheasant
Haiti: Hispaniolan trogon
Honduras: Yellow-naped Amazon parrot
Jamaica: Doctor bird hummingbird
Mexico: Golden eagle
Nicaragua: Turquoise-browed motmot
Panama: Harpy eagle
Puerto Rico: Bananaquit
St. Kitts and Nevis: Brown pelican
Trinidad: Scarlet ibis
Tobago: Cocrico

BIRDBRAINERS

What am I?
GFLAMO
Answer on page 153

THE ANCIENT TIMES OF NURSERY RHYMES

Goosey goosey gander, whither shall I wander, / Upstairs and downstairs and in my lady's chamber / There I met an old man who wouldn't say his prayers, / So I took him by the left leg and threw him down the stairs.

This childhood favourite emerges from the religious persecution of Catholics by Protestants, during which time searches of great houses were made in an attempt to find priests who disagreed with the new Book of Common Prayer, dig them out of their holes, and more often than not, kill them.

Others say that the rhyme originates during the Civil War, when Cromwell's troops scoured the old houses of England looking for royalists who wouldn't accept the new order. The Roundhead troops had a goose-stepping style of march.

WINGED WORDS

When I see a bird, I always look, wherever I am. It is no longer a conscious decision. I might be in the middle of a conversation of amazing importance about the Direction Of Our Marriage, but my eye will flick out of the window at a hint of movement, caught in the tail of my eye, and I will register: bloody hell, sparrowhawk. I might say it aloud, too – not necessarily a wise decision.

I once found a questionnaire in a birdwatching magazine. It asked: 'How often do you go birdwatching?' I reject the question out of hand. I don't go birdwatching. I am birdwatching. Birdwatching is a state of being, not an activity. It doesn't depend on place, on equipment, on specific purpose, like, say, fishing. It is not a matter of organic train-spotting; it is about life and it is about living.

Simon Barnes, *How to be a Bad Birdwatcher*, 2004

UK NUMBER ONE SINGLES
OF THE 50S, 60S AND 70S

Based on the charts published in New Musical Express

14/03/53	Guy Mitchell	*She Wears Red Feathers*
11/04/53	Stargazers	*Broken Wings*
21/11/64	The Rolling Stones	*Little Red Rooster* (2 weeks)
07/05/66	Manfred Mann	*Pretty Flamingo* (3 weeks)
25/01/69	Fleetwood Mac	*Albatross* (3 weeks)
26/06/71	Middle Of The Road	*Chirpy Chirpy Cheep Cheep* (5 weeks)

SING A SONG OF SEXINESS

Sometimes birds sing to attract mates. We all know that. But what exactly are the subtle differences in each individual song, and why do they matter?

A team of researchers at Cardiff University may have found the answer. Raising two sets of zebra finch chicks in separate ways – a healthy diet for one half, a restricted one for the other – they discovered that an important part of the birds' brains developed in two different ways.

Within a bird's brain lies its 'high vocal centre', a tiny structure just one third of a cubic millimetre in size that provides, if you like, an individual's singing talent. The chicks with the restricted diets developed smaller high vocal centres than those that were brought up more healthily.

In short, say the researchers, the better a male sings, the better it has been raised, suggesting that it might make a good mate.

The first Europeans to settle in North America encountered millions of Eskimo curlews (*Numenius borealis*), the continent's second most numerous shorebird. Yet today its very existence is uncertain. A sighting of more than 25 birds has not occurred since 1916, and the last confirmed report of even a single Eskimo curlew was over 40 years ago, in 1962.

Scientists disagree on the specific causes of this extraordinarily rapid decline, but it is clear that it is associated with the coming of the Europeans to the New World, and the population explosion that followed.

Most devastating for the curlew was the settlers' taste and technology for hunting. Known to many English-speakers as the Dough bird – owing to the thick layer of flesh it developed for migration – the curlew was thought a delicacy. In order to satisfy demand for the celebrated dark meat, they were hunted throughout the Americas (the Eskimo curlew wintered in Argentina) for 11 months of the year. Numbers began to dwindle significantly for the first time between 1870 and 1890, a period when hunting was completely unregulated in North America.

The curlew's natural temperament did nothing to counter its vulnerability; a tame and trusting species, the bird's response to an approaching human, be it conservationist or hunter, was to remain unalarmed and sit quite still.

What is more, it was the hospitable curlew itself who welcomed the Europeans to its home. After 65 days without sight of land, Christopher Columbus and his crew had been on the verge of abandoning the adventure westwards when they caught sight of a flock of birds. Immediately the ship's course was changed in the pursuit of the flock. Columbus' journal for the day (October 7 1492) explains that the birds were field birds, obviously incapable of finding rest on water, and modern analysis of migratory patterns show that the flock would probably have included Eskimo curlews.

In recent years the Eskimo curlew has achieved fame through Fred Bosworth's novelisation of a year in the life of one bird, following its remarkable 2,500 mile exodus from northern America to Argentina, and its search for a mate. *The Last of the Curlews* (1955; reissued 1998) was later adapted for an animated film, which was screened on US television in 1972 and won an Emmy award.

Bringing the curlew's plight to the public's attention has done little to arrest its decline, and a report published by the Saskatchewan Natural History Society in 1986 warned that the recovery of this species was unlikely. In 1981 however, there was an unconfirmed sighting of 23 Eskimo curlews in Texas – hope that we have not yet seen the last of Eskimo curlews after all.

Birds as observed by Gilbert White in his
Natural History of Selborne, 1788/9

From what follows, it will appear that neither owls nor cuckoos keep to one note. A friend remarks that many (most) of his owls hoot in B flat: but that one went almost half a note below A. The pipe he tried their notes by was a common half-crown pitch-pipe, such as masters use for tuning of harpsichords; it was the common London pitch.

A neighbour of mine, who is said to have a nice ear, remarks that the owls about this village hoot in three different keys, in G flat, or F sharp, in B flat and A flat. He heard two hooting to each other, the one in A flat, and the other in B flat. Query: Do these different notes proceed from different species, or only from various individuals? The same person finds upon trial that the note of the cuckoo (of which we have but one species) varies in different individuals; for, about Selborne wood, he found they were mostly in D: he heard two sing together, the one in D, the other in D sharp, who made a disagreeable concert: he afterwards heard one in D sharp, and about Wolmer-forest some in C. As to nightingales, he says that their notes are so short, and their transitions so rapid, that he cannot well ascertain their key. Perhaps in a cage, and in a room, their notes may be more distinguishable. This person has tried to settle the notes of a swift, and of several other small birds, but cannot bring them to any criterion.

THE CLASSIFIER CLASSIFIED

Sibley-Monroe is probably the most used and quoted avian classification system of modern times, its authors being two of the world's most respected taxonomists. When Burt Monroe died in 1994 aged just 63, much of the ornithological world went into mourning. Charles Sibley's death four years later was equally regretted, particularly for his scientific work. The man himself had been a legend, but like many committed naturalists, those around him didn't always feel bathed in the glow of a warming personality, as this excerpt from one obituary reveals:

'In argument he would bulldoze through, brooking no contradiction. Critics were baited with an acid tongue, and, in fits of temper, he could be a cruel mimic. In short, lesser mortals were not tolerated easily and, as has been said by others, collegiate friends were few. I never found him malicious or vindictive, even against those who had tried to bring him down. Nor was he particularly sophisticated or cultured, just a big, up-front Yank possessed by "the big picture" in avian phylogeny and convinced of the righteousness of his cause and invincibility of his intellect.'

[The owls] say the same thing over and over again so emphatically that I think it must be something nasty about me; but I shall not let myself be frightened away by the sarcasm of owls.
Elizabeth von Arnim, (born Mary Annette Beauchamp),
Elizabeth and her German Garden, 1898

BLUESBIRDS

BB Kingfisher
Muddy Waters' flufftail
Howlin' Wolf's wood-rail
Black bodiddlied woodpecker
John Mayallard
Bessie Smith's longspur

NB: Professor Longhair's real name was Henry Roeland 'Roy' Byrd

NB2: the lemon-bellied white-eye is not a blues singer... but should be

A SECOND LIFE

In 1981, Phoebe Snetsinger, a 50-year-old science teacher of Missouri USA, was told by a doctor that her cancer was terminal, and she had a year to live. Deciding not to bother with therapy, she set off for Alaska on a birdwatching trip she'd always wanted to take, the cancer went into remission, and from that initial death sentence sprang the most phenomenal of birdwatching careers.

Although the cancer returned periodically, Phoebe spent the next 18 years travelling the world and seeing more birds than anyone before or since. Chalking up a stunning life list of some 8,500 species, she scurried around the globe on expedition after expedition, funding her mission with an inheritance, her trademark floppy hat marking her presence wherever birds could be found.

As time passes, her life list will grow, as many of the subspecies she also saw gain species status in their own right. Yet obsessive list-building was not her only aim: she just loved to bird. 'Birding is the best and most exciting pursuit in the world, a glorified never-ending one,' she once said. 'And the whole experience of a foreign trip, whether you see 10 new birds or 500, is simply too good to miss.'

She died in Madagascar in 1999, having just seen a rare helmet vanga, but it was not the cancer that claimed her. The van in which she was travelling overturned, and she was killed instantly.

THE HOATZIN, NO HOAXIN'

Fight or flight: many creatures have special adaptations to help them achieve one or the other when in danger. The hoatzin, however, that red-eyed, blue-skinned, long-crested, clumsy flier of the South American rainforest canopy, can do both. If threatened the adult earns its alternative name of 'stink bird' by giving off a vile odour, the result of its leaf-eating habits that's best left to the imagination. The young aren't so competent at olfactory aggression, so they use a special run-away technique – they simply drop into the water below where they swim around for a bit. Then, once the danger has passed, they use the unique claw on the bend of each of their wings to help them climb back into the canopy.

Fight or flight? More like fart or fall.

NATIONAL TICKABILITY

The ten countries with the greatest number of breeding bird species

1.	Indonesia	929
2.	Colombia	708
3.	Peru	695
4.	Brazil	686
5.	China	618
6.	Venezuela	547
7.	Russia	528
8.	USA	508
9.	Bolivia	504
10.	India	458

BIRDS YOU MIGHT MYTH

If you're ever invited to come round for a meal of ziz, then know that your earthly time is up. According to Jewish lore, the meat of the ziz, the mightiest bird of them all, along with that of the behemoth and leviathan, will be consumed at the feast at the end of all times.

Until then, the ziz continues to do what it does best, protecting all the other birds of the air. It's big enough to do so, too: it is phenomenally strong, and can block out the light of the sun with its wings. Do not confuse this bird with the roc of Arab lands. Although rocs are similarly huge, there are more than one of them, and they have a habit of dropping mighty stones from above, described by silly scientists as 'meteorite showers'.

GIRLS WILL BE BOYS AND
BOYS WILL BE GIRLS

Polyandry, or the mating with more than one male by a single female, is rarely found in birds, but is one of the defining characteristics of the red-necked phalarope. In times when food is relatively scarce, the female will seek out more than one mate, leaving the various fathers behind to incubate the eggs. This reversal of usual roles is not just behavioural, it's reflected in the bird's plumage as well: it's the female that gets the looks in this bird, her bold rich markings contrasting heavily with the male's drabber paintwork.

Once the chicks are born, it is the male alone who broods them, thanks to his unusually well-developed prolactin secretions, normally a female hormone. To complete the gender-bending, the female's bright plumage is regulated by a healthy dose of testosterone.

But the unusualness of the phalarope does not stop there. They spend most of their life on the ocean, but unlike other birds with which they share these open spaces, they do not dive, because their down provides them with too high a degree of buoyancy. This makes them highly dependent on good feeding conditions, and is possibly the reason for their sexual role reversal, increasing the female's chances of successful breeding.

QUOTE UNQUOTE

People have been watching birds, in one way or another, since the first prehistoric hunter depicted his quarry on the walls of a cave.
Stephen Moss, writer and TV producer

MUCH BONDING IN THE MARSH

There's scandal afoot in the reedbed: male reed buntings are on the prowl. The birds have two different singing styles during the breeding season – although the notes are principally the same, single males sing faster than paired ones.

So what are the mated males doing? For a start, their slower version allows their song more individuality, allowing each female to identify easily which male is around. But the continued singing appears to have another message too: 'I may have been taken but, hey girls, I'm still available if you're interested'. It seems to work. A DNA analysis has shown that only 45% of reed bunting chicks are actually fathered by their mother's territorial mate.

Percentage of the world's threatened birds that can be found in just 5% of 75
the world's land surface

What an outrage it seemed! A cuckoo in a cage! ... Its mistress was hurt and a little offended at my protestations. No mortal bird upon this earth, she said, was every better treated. The children 'thought gold' of it, and fed it before feeding themselves at meal times ... They meant to keep it alive somehow, for the schoolmaster had promised them half a crown each if they still had it when the wild ones came. There was a saying that a caged cuckoo could not live the winter through, and, if this one did, he was going to write to the papers about it. Somebody at Birdwood had kept one till November once, but none had ever lived right over Christmas before in these parts...

For one wild moment I thought of outbidding the schoolmaster, but recollected in time that to do so would only be for it to exchange one prison for another, for to have freed it at such a season would have meant certain death. The only other thing I could think of was to present it with a roomier cage; but, while I was deciding whether it should be one of the circular wicker ones, known here as 'magpie cages', or something really substantial in wood and wire, news came that neither was any longer needed. A neighbour's cat had solved the problem by toppling its present one and destroying the inmate.

Flora Thompson, *A Country Calendar and other writings*, edited by Margaret Lane in 1979

BIRDBRAINERS

Which seabird am I?
upuffs upuffs
Answer on page 153

YOU CAN'T HAVE A BIRD BOOK WITHOUT PARROT JOKES

A man goes to an auction, where he sees a beautiful, exotic parrot. He really wants this bird, so he gets into the bidding. Although the bidding keeps rising, he hangs in there, until he's forced above his planned limit. Nonetheless, he's so taken with the bird, he keeps going until finally... sold! The parrot is his.

As he's paying for the bird, he says to the auctioneer: 'You know, I hope this parrot can talk. I've paid a lot of money for it, and it would be all worthwhile if he can say a word or two'.

'Don't worry', said the auctioneer, 'He can talk. Who do you think was bidding against you?'

BOOKS THAT MIGHT DISAPPOINT
THE HOPEFUL ORNITHOLOGIST

Swallows and Amazons,
by Arthur Ransome
Actually about kids in boats

Where Eagles Dare,
by Alastair MacLean
Actually about crafty wartime manoeuvres

Birdsong, by Sebastian Faulks
Actually about war again

The Peregrine Spy,
by Edmund P Murray
Actually about espionage in Iran

Phoenix Cardinals,
by Richard Rambeck
Actually about American football

Nightingale's Lament,
by Simon R Green
Actually about a London siren

The Sparrow,
by Mary Doria Russell
Actually about a planet called Rakhat

Mr Vogel, by Lloyd Jones
Actually about Wales

RESERVOIR DUCKS

Mr Whitebacked Vulture
Mr Orange Bullfinch
Mr Pink Cockatoo
Mr Blond Crested Woodpecker
Mr Blue Tit
Also featuring Quentin Tarantino as Mr Brown Babbler

WWT FOR ALL

The Wildfowl & Wetlands Trust is the largest international wetland conservation charity in the UK. Founded in 1946 by the artist and naturalist Sir Peter Scott (1909 – 1989), WWT has nine visitor centres around the UK, where people can get closer to wetland birds and enjoy spectacular wetland landscapes.

Membership of the Trust brings the following privileges:
- Membership pack, including WWT brochure, window sticker and reduced entry vouchers for family and friends
- Quarterly delivery of Wildfowl and Wetland, WWT's membership magazine
- Reduced rates on WWT events.
- Free entry to all WWT centres.

For further information, call 01453 891915, or email membership@wwt.org.uk

Bill's out of

&

*and uses this to get
his brogues off*

(8 letters)
Answer on page 153

BORN TO LOVE BIRDS

Probably best known for his *Age of Fable*, Thomas Bulfinch (1796–1867) was a chronicler of the myths and tales of ancient religions, Charlemagne and King Arthur, his aim being to enlighten 'the reader of English literature, of either sex, who wishes to comprehend the allusions so frequently made by public speakers, lecturers, essayists, and poets, and those which occur in polite conversation'. Yet before completing *Bulfinch's Mythology* (as the collection is now known), this Harvard-educated son of a Massachusetts architect spent much of the 1840s as the secretary of the Boston Society of Natural History.

The Society was a forum for many prominent scientists of the day, and his six-year stint there, which began with an interest in birds and other wildlife, made him aware of the rapid expansion of scientific knowledge that the age was enjoying. This worried him. He feared that scientific reliance might become a threat to the role of the classics in broadening education, and his mighty work began. Today, in many parts of America, it is still viewed as the standard classical reference work for teachers.

Any chance that the official names of the spotted redshank, bar-tailed godwit or grasshopper warbler will become spotshank, barwit or gropper in the future, just as they're nicknamed today? If the pomarine skua is anything to go by, it's a possibility.

Pomarine is a contraction of the bird's original name, pomatorhine, which means flap-nose, referring to the bird's bony structure across the nostril. Pomatorhine being a bit of a mouthful, the contracted version became standard as the 20th century wore on.

But this is only the beginning of the story. The naming of skuas in general seems to be an ever-changing affair. In 1891, when Cornelius Brown wrote his History of Nottinghamshire, he listed the 246 species that had been recorded to date in the county. This list included the common skua, Richardson's skua and Buffon's skua, along with the aforementioned pomatorhine skua. None of these birds is so named today. The common skua has become great, Richardson's is now Arctic, and Buffon's is the long-tailed.

The Richardson referred to was John (1787–1865), a Scottish naturalist, surgeon and Arctic explorer who worked with Northwest Passage discoverer John Franklin and was part of the expeditions to find him in the mid-19th century. Meanwhile, Georges Louis Leclerc, Comte de Buffon, (1707–1788) was a French naturalist whose writings went some way towards developing the understanding of the concept of species.

Just to add to the confusion, the Arctic skua is more frequently known today as the parasitic skua, based on its habit of harrying other birds until they drop their food. The great skua, too, is as often known by its northern Scottish isles name of bonxie as by its English name.

So four birds, and 10 names. But there's more. The word skua comes from skufr, which was the old Norse name for the bird. It means, broadly speaking, brown gull, and perhaps derives from an onomatopoeic reference to its call. Thing is, they don't call them skuas in America. They call them jaegers, from the German for hunter. Except that is, for the great, or common skua, or bonxie. They simply call that one the skua. Oh, in Yorkshire, however, it's sometimes called jager.

The aspirins are in the medicine cabinet behind you.

QUOTE UNQUOTE

I hope you love birds too. It is economical. It saves going to heaven.
Emily Dickinson, poet

I cannot tell whether I were more pleased or mortified to observe, in those solitary walks, that the smaller birds did not appear to be at all afraid of me, but would hop about within a yard's distance, looking for worms and other food, with as much indifference and security as if no creature at all were near them. I remember, a thrush had the confidence to snatch out of my hand, with his bill, a piece of cake that Glumdalclitch had just given me for my breakfast. When I attempted to catch any of these birds, they would boldly turn against me, endeavouring to peck my fingers, which I durst not venture within their reach; and then they would hop back unconcerned, to hunt for worms or snails, as they did before. But one day, I took a thick cudgel, and threw it with all my strength so luckily, at a linnet, that I knocked him down, and seizing him by the neck with both my hands, ran with him in triumph to my nurse. However, the bird, who had only been stunned, recovering himself gave me so many boxes with his wings, on both sides of my head and body, though I held him at arm's-length, and was out of the reach of his claws, that I was twenty times thinking to let him go. But I was soon relieved by one of our servants, who wrung off the bird's neck, and I had him next day for dinner, by the queen's command. This linnet, as near as I can remember, seemed to be somewhat larger than an English swan.

Jonathan Swift, *Gulliver's Travels*, 1726. Lemuel Gulliver has reached Brobdingnag.

I CAN SING A RAINBOW

Red kite • Orange chat
Yellow weaver • Green hermit
Blue crane • Indigo bunting
Violet cuckoo

WHAT'S IN A NAME?

Oddly enough, for a bird often described as mute, the swan gets its name from an old Germanic base swanaz, meaning singer, or one who makes sound. Probably coming from the remarkable sound that several bugling whoopers can make as they gather in the dying winter months, the bird became a symbol of melody and joy as a being enters the afterlife. Homer and Chaucer both alluded to the swan's song, and the phrase became particularly associated with a person's dying act when Schubert completed his final song cycle, Schwanengesang, just before his death in 1828.

Each year, the American Birding Association backs a mighty 24-hour birdwatching bonanza in an attempt to find America's birdiest city and county. The tournament, held in May, pits Audubon Society and birdwatching club members against each other across the continent to discover who can count the greatest number of species in a day.

It was New York who started the whole thing off, proudly describing themselves as America's Birdiest City in 2001 when a 24-hour watchathon produced 185 species. Since laying down the gauntlet, as the table of 2004 winners shows, their measly total has been thumped... typically, by the Texans.

Category	Locale	Totals
Large city, coastal	Corpus Christi, TX	241
Large city, inland	Chicago, IL	168
Small city, coastal	Brownsville, TX	125
Small city, inland	Duluth, MN	166
Coastal county, western	San Diego, CA	266
Coastal county, eastern	Kings, NY	163
Inland county, western	Kern, CA	232
Inland county, eastern	Cook, IL	199

TALKING TURKEY

Turkeys are social birds and in winter separate into three distinct groups: adult males (toms), young males (jakes), and females (hens).

Wild turkeys can fly for short distances up to 55 miles per hour, and can run at speeds up to 20 miles per hour. During the spring, a male wild turkey's physical appearance changes: his head turns a brilliant red, white and blue. Turkeys can see in colour but have poor night vision.

Wild turkey populations fell to fewer than 30,000 birds by the 1930s due to habitat destruction and unregulated shooting. Today, there are over 6 million in the wild.

During US Air Force test runs in breaking the sound barrier, nearby turkeys dropped dead with heart attacks.

Benjamin Franklin disapproved of the bald eagle as America's national bird, preferring instead the turkey. 'The turkey is a much more respectable bird, and a true original native of America. He is besides, though a little vain and silly, a bird of courage, and would not hesitate to attack a grenadier of the British Guards who should presume to invade his farmyard with a red coat on.'

So just what was that partridge doing up a pear tree anyway? The Latin for partridge is Perdix, one of the sacred kings of Athena, who was thrown to his death from a high tower. Athena turned him into a bird, and because of his love for her, raised him from the dead and carried him in the branches of a tree to the heavens. As Athena was the mother of all pear trees (now that's a title we'd all love to have), it was such a tree that bore poor Perdix.

As the lifting of the Perdix the partridge reminded many of the resurrection of Christ, the symbolism eventually switched in religious tone. Some believe that the Twelve Days of Christmas are religious code, used during times when outspoken Christianity did little other than get you killed. So the partridge was Jesus; the two turtle doves the Old Testament and Hebrew scripture (doves being sacred birds); the three French hens represented the three virtues (hens being habitual birds in their behaviour); Matthew, Mark, Luke and John who told the full story of Jesus were turned into four calling birds (or colly birds, ie blackbirds, who sing through the day and night). The six days of creation turn into geese a-laying, while the seven gifts of the Holy Spirit become beautiful swans.

Just to complete the dozen, the five gold rings are the first books of the Bible, the eight maids a-milking are the Beatitudes, and the nine fruits of the Holy Spirit become dancing ladies. Ten Leaping Lords match the Commandments, the 11 pipers are the faithful apostles who continued to spread the word, and the soulful drummers beat out the 12 doctrines in the Apostles' Creed.

THE STORIES BEHIND THE BIRDS OF HOLLYWOOD

When Jonathan Livingston Seagull, a short novella about a gull who finds his own spiritual path and exceeds his physical limits, hit best-seller status and became virtually illegal not to read in the early 1970s, the movie could not be far away. It duly arrived in 1973, and promptly lived up to its purist roots. Richard D Bach, the author, sued the production for veering too far away from his text, while Neil Diamond, brought on board to provide the intense moodiness beloved of the era, sued because the overall score was changed.

So after a brief sojourn with spiritual Zenlike awareness, JLS returned to the earthly claims of Mammon.

And the audience felt gulled. As one critic said: 'Livingston? Living hell'.

MARVELLOUS MERCENARIES

Marvel comics are well known for many of their superheroes, whose exploits under the names of Spider-Man, the Hulk, the X-Men and Captain America have entered pulp legend. Of considerably lesser fame, however, was a group of mercenaries called Air Force who briefly plied their trade within comics during the 90s, who could fly, and whose monikers were based on bird names. The list included:

Killer Shrike   Mean flier, with nifty little wrist blades

Cardinal   Great at aerial combat, and a fine marksman

Oriole   Martial arts expert

Tanager   Aerial combat specialist. That was about it

Sparrow   No, really. Her name was Sparrow. You'd think Hawk or Eagle or something but no, she was Sparrow.

BIRDBRAINERS

Which game bird is a woman's name followed by a man's name?
Answer on page 153

BROLGA KORBUT

The brolga, Australia's stately blue-grey crane, has a special niche in Aboriginal folklore, due to its magnificent and graceful dance. According to the tales from dreamtime, Brolga was a young, beautiful woman who could dance like no other, imitating even the wind in her fluid movements. People came from far away to watch her, and although her fellow tribes-people worried that the attention might go to her head, it never did.

One day, she went out on the plain to dance alone, where an evil spirit whipped her away in a whirlwind, or willywilly. Even her footprints were gone, and none could find her, as she had swirled up to the sky. But shortly afterwards, a tall bird arrived, stretching its wings and dancing just as Brolga had done. The people realised that their beloved girl had escaped the spirit and returned to earth in the form of a bird.

The actual dance of the crane itself is one of true grace. It begins when a bird picks up some grass and tosses it into the air, catching it while leaping. Its mate usually joins in, and the pair begin stretching, calling, bowing and bobbing their heads. The most spectacular sight is when the dancing frenzy grips several of the birds at one time, as they line up facing each other and launch themselves into a whirling, leaping, bobbing salute.

The rail family, containing several flightless species, has been one of the hardest hit in recent centuries, as this list of extinct species shows:

Chatham Islands rail, *Rallus modestus*
Wake Island rail, *Rallus wakensis*
Tahitian red-billed rail, *Rallus pacificus*
Ascension Island rail, *Atlantisia elpenor*
Kusaie Island crake, *Porzana monasa*
Hawaiian rail, *Porzana sandwichensis*
Laysan rail, *Porzana palmeri*
Samoan wood rail, *Gallinula pacifica*
Lord Howe swamphen, *Porphyrio albus*
Mauritius red hen, *Aphanapteryx bonasia*
Leguat's gelinote, *Aphanapteryx leguatz*

QUOTE UNQUOTE

The larks were everywhere. No individual bird could be disentangled. The song of one knitted into the rolling pattern of its neighbour to form a seamless web of music – one glorious anthem that rose upwards in great vaults to roof the heaven with an indeterminate architecture of sound.
Mark Cocker, bird writer

LAST CHANCE?

The po'ouli, quite possibly the rarest bird in the world, is still hanging in there. For several years, only three individuals of this Hawaiian honeycreeper with the black mask have remained, each living in a different part of Hawaii's Maui forest. The trouble was, each one of them seemed unaware of the others' existence, and despite attempts to bring them together, the unfortunate state of ignorance continued.

There was only one hope left: see if they would breed in captivity. First, however, you have to catch your po'ouli. After months of trying, a recovery team finally caught one of them in October 2004, and then set about trying to get hold of the other two individuals. They're small birds, however, they call very rarely, and the Maui forest is very large. Needles and haystacks come to mind.

And then the worst happened. The bird that Kirsty Swinnerton and her po'ouli recovery team caught – a male – died in December 2004.

As this book went to print, the hunt was on for the two remaining po'ouli... and a mini-miracle.

Number of eggs eaten by Tsar Peter the Great and his party while dining at Godalming's Kings Arms Royal Hotel in 1689. The bill remains unpaid

The grand old duke of squawk
Nursery rhyme

DEAD RINGERS

If you find a dead bird with a ring on it, you can send the details to the British Trust for Ornithology (The Nunnery, Thetford, Norfolk, United Kingdom IP24 2PU), stating:

- your full name
- your postal address
- the species (if known)
- the metal ring number (read from left to right from the split in the ring). State the address if not a BTO or British Museum ring.
- the location the bird was found including the name of the nearest town or village, county and a grid reference if possible
- the exact day, month and year it was found. If not known please approximate as closely as you can
- the cause of death (if known)
- how long the bird has been dead (if known).

The BTO will send you the bird's details within approximately one month. If you send the ring with your letter, it will be returned if requested.

WINGED WORDS

One morning in the late summer, I noticed a few purple martins, large, beautiful swallows common in that region, engaged, at a considerable height, in the aerial exercises in which they pass so much of their time each day. By and by one of the birds separated itself from the others, and, circling slowly downward, finally alighted on the ground not far from me. ...It made no movement when I approached to within four yards of it; and after I had stood still at that distance for a minute or so, attentively regarding it, I saw it put out one wing and turn over on its side. I at once took it up in my hand, and found that it was already quite dead. ...I concluded that it was an old bird that had died solely from natural failure of the life-energy.

But how wonderful, how almost incredible, that the healthy vigour and joy of life should have continued in this individual bird down to within so short a period of the end; that it should have been not only strong enough to find its food, but to rush and wheel about for long intervals in purely sportive exercises, when the brief twilight of decline and final extinction were so near!

WH Hudson, *Birds in a Village,* **1898**

THE BIRDS: THE REMAKE

Starring:
Mia Sparrow
Meryl Cheep
Harrier Ford
Bird Lancaster
Sandra Bullfinch
Tom Crows

Directed by Alfred Spatchcock

ONLY A POOR LITTLE SPARROW

The sporting world's most famous sparrow is undoubtedly the individual stuffed and mounted in the MCC Museum at the home of cricket, Lord's. The poor creature had the misfortune in 1936 to be crossing the ground, flying low, just as Jehangir Khan let fly with one of his deliveries.

Birds seemed to follow Jehangir around. He only played four tests for India, but in the second innings of his debut test, coincidentally at Lords in 1932, he was bowled by Bill Voce for a golden duck. And in his second innings of the 1936 Lord's test, he was out for 13 caught by... George Duckworth.

THE ANCIENT TIMES OF NURSERY RHYMES

Sing a song of sixpence, a pocketful of rye
Four and twenty blackbirds baked in a pie
When the pie was opened the birds began to sing
Wasn't that a dainty dish to set before the king

In the 16th century, court cooks would sometimes bake a pie, then remove the contents and replace them with songbirds. They weren't intended as food, but as entertainment, and this nursery rhyme could be a simple description of the way that ordinary folk believed that royals lived.

Or could it? The famous pirate, Blackbeard, was known for paying his men the decent wage of sixpence and a pouch of alcohol. His ship would often sail disguised as a trading vessel, until it got close enough to one of the king's ships, whereupon the pirates – perhaps two dozen or more – would leap forth and plunder merrily.

Which version do you prefer? Thought so.

NOT REALLY

Mute swan	Can actually hiss and snort
Bearded reedling	More of a moustache, really
Marsh tit	Principally a woodland bird
Spotted flycatcher	Streaked, rather than spotted (except the juv)
Dartford warbler	You're better off looking for it further west
Snow bunting	Oh yes 'tis

WREN AND SCRIMPING

From 1672 to 1936, Britannia didn't just rule the waves, but the farthing as well. Her image appeared on the reverse side of this quarter-penny coin (value in decimalisation: 0.104167 of 1p) throughout this era until 1937 when she was overthrown by... the wren. The smallness and familiarity of the little bird gave the coin an endearing quality until its last production in 1956, and removal from circulation at the end of 1960.

And for those who pointed out that the goldcrest and firecrest are actually smaller than the wren, the Royal Mint had an answer. Although they were no longer in circulation, half-farthings, third-farthings and even quarter-farthings had existed in the 19th century, largely (if that's the right word) for use in the colonies.

The good woman had risen thus early (for as yet it was scarcely sunrise) in order to set about making a scarecrow, which she intended to put in the middle of her corn-patch. It was now the latter week of May, and the crows and blackbirds had already discovered the little, green, rolledup leaf of the Indian corn just peeping out of the soil. She was determined, therefore, to contrive as lifelike a scarecrow as ever was seen, and to finish it immediately, from top to toe, so that it should begin its sentinel's duty that very morning. Now Mother Rigby (as everybody must have heard) was one of the most cunning and potent witches in New England, and might, with very little trouble, have made a scarecrow ugly enough to frighten the minister himself. But on this occasion, as she had awakened in an uncommonly pleasant humor, and was further dulcified by her pipe tobacco, she resolved to produce something fine, beautiful, and splendid, rather than hideous and horrible.

'I don't want to set up a hobgoblin in my own corn-patch, and almost at my own doorstep,' said Mother Rigby to herself, puffing out a whiff of smoke; 'I could do it if I pleased, but I'm tired of doing marvellous things, and so I'll keep within the bounds of every-day business just for variety's sake. Besides, there is no use in scaring the little children for a mile roundabout, though 't is true I'm a witch.'

Nathaniel Hawthorne, *Feathertop: A Moralised Legend*, 1851

QUOTE UNQUOTE

I am but mad north-north-west: when the wind is southerly I know a hawk from a handsaw.
William Shakespeare, *Hamlet*

ANDY IN A CRISIS

Attentive parenting is one thing, but in 2004 Andy, an Andean flamingo at the WWT Slimbridge headquarters, took fatherhood to the next stage. He spent several days incubating a pebble.

The likelihood for this unusual behaviour was that a gull or crow took the egg that Andy's mate had laid. Once the female had left the nest, Andy must have noticed a large pebble that still lay there, and thinking that it was the egg took over the incubation duties.

Staff eventually replaced the pebble with a wooden egg to keep the bird interested, in case another female rejected her own egg for some reason, and it could then be swopped for Andy's.

• According to Mayan legend the hummingbird is the sun in disguise, the little bird being made from the scraps left over when the gods created the other birds. The gods were so pleased with what they'd done, they held a huge wedding ceremony for the hummingbirds to which all the creatures contributed, but the guests noticed that the brilliantly hued little groom became drab whenever he turned away from the sun.

• The Chayma people of Trinidad have another view of hummingbirds: they see them as representatives of their dead ancestors who thus cannot be harmed.

• The Caribbean tribe of the Arawacs believed that it was the hummingbird, or doctor bird as they called it, that brought tobacco to earth. As the Arawacs are now extinct, one wonders if there might be a connection.

• The Pueblo also connected the hummingbird with tobacco, the little bird collecting smoke from the caterpillar who guards the plant, and bringing it to the shamans who use it to purify the earth. According to the Pueblo, the hummingbird also saved the world when a volcano demon tried to destroy it with hot lava. The hummingbird gathered together the clouds of the skies and used them to put out the fire. In the process, while dashing through a rainbow, he gained the bright colours he still wears today.

• The Puerto Rican Jatibonicu people tell a Romeo and Juliet story of two young people from rival tribes who fell into forbidden love. To escape the wrath of their peoples, they turned themselves, respectively, into the hummingbird and the flower.

• A Cherokee story tells of a woman who was loved by both a hummingbird and a crane. Although she chooses the former, the crane convinces her that the two birds should race around the world for her hand. She agrees, thinking that the little hummer will win, but unlike the crane, he cannot fly at night, so he loses. Unable to accept the victory of the crane, she takes neither bird.

• According to Mojave legend, mankind once lived in an underground world of darkness. It was the little hummingbird who found the convoluted path up to the surface world. The people followed, and live in sunlight to this day.

• The Navajo went one step further, sending the hummingbird up to see what lay beyond the blue sky itself. He found nothing.

- Hopi people to this day paint hummingbirds on water jars, to thank the little birds for bringing rain. One legend has two little children during a time of famine who make a toy hummingbird which comes to life, flies to the centre of the earth, and pleads with the god of fertility to make it rain, which duly happens.

- The hummingbird as messenger also spills over into the Noah legend. The Pima people gave the little flier the role of the dove in their flood story, bringing back a flower to show that the waters had subsided.

- Sometimes, the help goes the other way. When a Taroscan woman of Mexico gave sugar water to a dying hummingbird during a drought, the bird was so grateful that he taught her how to weave beautiful baskets. These baskets are still made today for Day of the Dead festivals.

- The Aztecs, who used to use hummingbird feathers in their head-dresses, had a special relationship with the bird. There was once a brave warrior named Huitzilopochtli, or 'hummingbird who came from the left', who led the Aztecs to a new homeland and defended it for them. Then, one day he was killed in a great battle. A tiny green hummingbird rose from where he had fallen and inspired his followers to fight on,

which they did, to victory. The warrior was turned into a god, and all warriors who fell thereafter were lifted to the sun for four years before returning as hummingbirds. Every night, they would turn back into soldiers and fight back the powers of darkness, allowing the sun to rise again each morning. The hummingbird had a gentle side, too. It was the form taken by the god of music and poetry when he descended to the underworld. There, he made love with a goddess, and the fruits of their love became the very first flower.

- An Apache legend merges the warrior with the romantic. Wind Dancer, a great fighter, was completely deaf but capable of singing magical songs that could heal and bring good weather. Among his many deeds was the rescue from the clutches of a wolf of Bright Rain, a beautiful young woman who he later married. Their marriage did not last long: Wind Dancer was killed in battle soon afterwards, bringing a terrible winter to ravage the lands. Bright Rain began taking herself off for long, solitary walks, and before long the winter ended as abruptly as it had begun. It transpired that Wind Dancer had been appearing to her during her walks in the form of a hummingbird, wearing his bright ceremonial war paint, and whispering his songs into her ear.

QUOTE UNQUOTE

No bird soars too high if he soars with his own wings
William Blake, poet

Mix the result for not godwit but Godhit

What's the word?
Answer on page 153

ABSOLUTELY FABULOUS

The Swallow and the Crow, by Aesop
The swallow and the crow had a contention about their plumage. The crow put an end to the dispute by saying, 'Your feathers are all very well in the spring, but mine protect me against the winter.'
Fair weather friends are not worth much.

MUD, MUD, GLORIOUS MUD

Climate change can affect birds in many ways, and sometimes it requires a little lateral thinking to work out the reasons. The house martin, for example, has been in steady decline in parts of central Europe for many years, falling by 38% in Britain since 1970. Although part of that reason is due to pollution and the reduction of insect numbers by pesticides, the birds are greatly affected by the weather... or lack of it. Without rain, there's less mud, and as this is the prime material they use for nest-building, as well as a great encouragement for breeding insects, hotter springs appear to have severely affected their numbers.

Depth, in metres, at which a diving guillemot has been recorded in the North Sea 91

Superspy and suave sophisticate James Bond, as most trivia buffs know, was a product of ornithology. His creator, Ian Fleming, nicked the name from a copy of *Birds of the West Indies*, James Bond being the author. Fleming felt the moniker was 'brief, unromantic, masculine and Anglo-Saxon. Just what I needed'.

The original, a Philadelphia-born ornithologist (1900-1989), didn't mind too much, but occasionally resented the unwanted intrusion into his life from his new and inevitable fan-base. His wife Mary, however, knew how to make light of it. She once wrote to Ian Fleming half jokingly threatening to sue. 'I must confess that your husband has every reason to sue me,' came back the reply. 'In return, I can only offer your James Bond unlimited use of the name Ian Fleming for any purpose he may think fit.' In fact, Fleming and Bond did meet once (ironically at Goldeneye, Fleming's home), and the former asked the latter if, should he discover a new species, he would name it after the spy-writer. Bond did not discover any.

In 1980, Mary kept the link going, and published a biography of her husband. She called it *To James Bond with Love*.

BIRDBRAINERS

What am I?
ACARDL
Answer on page 153

MUTE SWANS AND THE OLD BILL

- The bird was given royal status in the 12th century, and by 1378 the office of 'Keeper of the King's Swans' was introduced.
- A 1482/3 document entitled 'The Lawes, Orders and Customs for Swans' lays down that all swans previously owned by those who pay less than five marks a year freehold, are forfeit to the king.
- Swan-upping, or marking cygnets' bills with the same symbol as carried by their parents, was completed in one day in Elizabethan times, the levy being 6s 8d.
- Although not strictly a conservation measure, more a right of property, theft of the eggs was punishable by up to one year's imprisonment. Meanwhile, anyone who was not a swanherd, but who owned a swan hook, was liable to a fine of 13s 4d.
- The pub sign 'Swan with two necks' refers in fact to the nicks in its bill, a symbol of the Worshipful Company of Vintners.

THE ULTIMATE ANNIVERSARY PRESENT?

Although some of the following have dropped the 'Mrs', or are better known by other names, each was initially named after his wife by the naturalist who discovered it.

Mrs Benson's warbler
Mrs Boulton's woodland warbler
Mrs Forbes-Watson's black flycatcher
Mrs Gould's sunbird
Mrs Hume's pheasant
Mrs Moreau's warbler
Mrs Swinhoe's sunbird
Mrs Vernay's blood pheasant

There is also a subspecies of the crowned lapwing which sounds as if it belongs to someone's wife: *Vanellus coronatus demissus*.

WINGED WORDS

Soon I hear the all-pervading hum of an approaching hummingbird circling above the rock, which afterward I mistake several times for the gruff voices of men approaching, unlike as these sounds are in some respects, and I perceive the resemblance even when I know better. Now I am sure it is a hummingbird, and now that it is two farmers approaching. But presently the hum becomes more sharp and thrilling, and the little fellow suddenly perches on an ash twig within a rod of me, and plumes himself while the rain is fairly beginning. He is quite out of proportion to the size of his perch. It does not acknowledge his weight.

HD Thoreau's journal, 29 May 1857

WELL OIL BE

The oilbird of South America is by no means the only nocturnal bird in the world, but it is the only one that eats fruit. Plenty of it, too. Remaining at their cave-based nesting sites all day, every day, the oilbird leaves at dusk in search of the fruit of palms and laurels which it devours or, during the extended breeding season, brings back to its young in great numbers. The nests themselves are made of regurgitated seeds, and grow year by year, while the young gorge themselves during their four-month stay in the nest, attaining sizes up to 50% larger than their parents.

The bird was given its name by Alexander von Humboldt, who in 1799 witnessed local people taking the chubby nestlings and boiling down their fat to use as oil for their torches and cooking.

Number of years between previous sighting of the grey-throated leaftosser on Tobago, and its rediscovery there in 1996   93

WHAT'S IN A NAME?

The second half of magpie is easy to define: it comes from the bird's Latin name, *Pica*, which, like the *Picus* (woodpecker) refers to the sharp dagger-like quality of the bill. The first half... well, that's slightly harder to explain in this more enlightened age. Mag is a contraction of Margaret, a common 16th century name that was often used to denote women in general, and qualities associated with women. The 'female quality' that was recognised in the magpie was... its idle chatter.

Please don't shoot the messenger.

A LEXICOLOGY OF ORNITHOLOGY'S OLOGIES

Caliology . . . . Study of nests
Cryptoornithology . . . . Study of mythical birds
Neossology . . . . Study of nestlings
Nidology . . . . Also the study of nests
Oology . . . . Study of eggs
Ovology . . . . Also the study of eggs
Palaeoornithology . . . . Study of fossilised birds
Pterylology . . . . Study of feather arrangements on a bird
Theriogenology . . . . Study of reproductive systems

DOWN THE HATCH

If you should ever find yourself staring at the contents of a grebe's stomach (goodness knows why, but bear with this), you might get the impression that the bird had turned itself inside out. Its stomach could be up to 50% full of feathers. In fact, even young grebes just a few days old snack happily on their parents' down.

The reason for this extraordinary behaviour is the birds' diet. Primarily fish-eaters, grebes do not possess sufficiently strong gizzards to crush the fish bones on the way down, so the balls of feathers that they accumulate in their stomachs both protect the stomach walls and trap the bones, allowing the digestive juices to dissolve them before they pass into the intestine.

All of which suggests that grebes, among the most ancient of birds, were not great fish eaters in their early days, and as they expanded their diet have found their own way of overcoming an evolutionary inadequacy.

We think caged birds sing, when indeed they cry.
John Webster, Jacobean playwright

WHY DID THE OWL 'OWL?

Owls still need protection today, but at least they don't suffer the indignities of the past, as the following shows:

- The birds were thought in the Middle Ages to be able to cure alcoholism. Swallowing their eggs whole could reputedly save the drunkest of the drunkards.
- Their eyeballs were believed to ward off evil if worn round the neck in Morocco, or eaten in India.
- Owl soup was drunk by the Romans as a cure for epilepsy.
- A similar broth prevented Middle Ages children from contracting whooping cough.
- A dried owl's foot placed in a cot brought childhood health, according to Germans of the Middle Ages.
- India again, and stewed eyeballs and brains were believed to reduce labour pains.
- 16th century Swiss doctors recommended jellied owl brains as a cure for constipation.
- Back to ancient Rome, and insect bites could be eased by a poultice of owl meat.

BECAUSE THE WOODPECKER
WOULD PECK 'ER

The lesser spotted woodpecker is in decline, its numbers tumbling faster than the average woodland specialist. A number of reasons have been put forward, including the bird's possible inability to adapt to the loss of elm trees that once supported it, and the tendency to clear rotting wood from woodland that helps provide the insects that sustain the little woodpecker.

But could it be that there's some internecine rivalry going on? The great spotted woodpecker, conversely, is doing very well, partly because it has adapted to garden handouts and urban settings. Could it be that it's beginning to force out its diminutive cousin? Records have often shown the larger of the pied woodpeckers driving the smaller from their nests, a practice sustainable while lesser spots still retain reasonable population levels, but one that can become critical once the population falls below a certain point.

If so, this could be among the first recorded avian examples of one native and widespread cousin endangering another.

TREE GOOD REASONS

Until 1871 there was no record of tree-nesting ducks in Britain. That was the year that the first breeding goosander were recorded, in Perthshire, and since then they've been joined by the Mandarin duck and the goldeneye, each a successful tree-hole user. Now, the Mandarin is an introduced species and so there's no surprise that it didn't take to British breeding earlier, but why did it take so long for the other two birds to settle in?

Wildfowl expert and former WWT Director of Centres Janet Kear believes it could be a combination of three factors:

- The increasing number of nestboxes put out by the public and conservation bodies has helped compensate for the relatively limited number of large holes in British trees (our woodpeckers tend to drill holes too small for ducks)
- The decline of the pine marten, a tree-climber and egg-stealer, has allowed the birds to flourish
- Climate change may mean that the species, which are early nesters, have more success.

HIGH AMBITIONS, CANADIAN-STYLE

A list of peaks in the Canadian Rockies that mountain-climbing birdwatchers might want to try:

Aquila Mountain
Crowsnest Mountain
Eagle Ridge
Golden Eagle Peak
Hawk Ridge
Pigeon Mountain
Ptarmigan Peak
Whitecrow Mountain

PHONETICALLY SPEAKING

How the Collins Bird Guide *(CBG),* Bill Oddie's Birds of Britain and Ireland, *(BOB),* RSPB Handbook of British Birds *(HBB) and* Observer's Book of Birds *(OBB) hear the sea birds.*

Sandwich tern: kerrick (CBG); kirrick (BOB); keer-ick (HBB); tre-wit (OBB)

Kittiwake: kitt-i-waake (CBG); kitti wake (BOB); kitti waaark (HBB); kittiwake (OBB)

Eider: a-ooh-e (CBG); oo oo oo (BOB); ar-oooo (HBB); coo (OBB)

96 *Percentage of dead fulmars analysed from the North Sea found with plastic in their stomachs*

A nightingale, that all day long
Had cheered the village with his song,
Nor yet at eve his note suspended,
Nor yet when eventide was ended,
Began to feel, as well he might,
The keen demands of appetite;
When, looking eagerly around,
He spied far off, upon the ground,
A something shining in the dark,
And knew the glow-worm by his spark;
So, stooping down from hawthorn top,
He thought to put him in his crop.
The worm, aware of his intent,
Harangued him thus, right eloquent:
'Did you admire my lamp,' quoth he,
'As much as I your minstrelsy,
You would abhor to do me wrong,
As much as I to spoil your song;
For 'twas the self-same Power Divine
Taught you to sing, and me to shine;
That you with music, I with light,
Might beautify, and cheer the night.'
The songster heard this short oration,
And, warbling out his approbation,
Released him, as my story tells,
And found a supper somewhere else.

William Cowper (1731-1800),
The Nightingale and the Glow-worm

GOOD OLD BIRDS

Highest recorded ages for common British birds include:

Common tern	33
Puffin	30
Grey heron	23
Lapwing	21
Dunlin	18
Green woodpecker	15
Blackbird	14
House sparrow	12
Swallow	11

Britain's oldest bird to date is a Manx shearwater, aged at least 52 in 2003.

Number recorded in Lincolnshire during the 2000 invasion of the honey buzzards 97

YOU CAN'T HAVE A BIRD BOOK
WITHOUT PARROT JOKES

A woman takes a limp parrot to the vet. She lays her pet on the table, and the vet pulls out his stethoscope, listens to the bird's chest then shakes his head. 'I'm so sorry, Polly has passed away.'

'Are you sure?' cries the woman. 'Couldn't you run some tests?' The vet shrugs, opens a door, and in come a black labrador and a cat. The dog stands on its hind legs, and sniffs the bird from top to bottom, then looks at the vet and shakes his head. Then the cat jumps onto the table, and gazes at the parrot, sniffing occasionally, before looking at the vet and shaking its head too.

'Proof' says the vet. 'I'm afraid your parrot is most certainly dead. That'll be £150 please.'

'£150' cries the owner. 'Just to tell me my bird is dead?'

'No,' says the vet. 'My time costs just £20. The extra £130 is for the lab report and the cat scan.'

THE ANCIENT TIMES OF NURSERY RHYMES

Who killed Cock Robin
I said the sparrow
With my bow and arrow
I killed cock robin

...All the birds of the air
fell a-sighing and a-sobbing
When they heard of the death
of poor Cock Robin

The origins of this list of avian mourners probably lie in Norse legend. When Balder, the son of Odin and the most handsome, wise and beloved of all the gods, dreamed of his own death, his sister Frigg, toured the lands exacting promises from all creatures and plants that they would not hurt him. Unfortunately, she ignored the mistletoe, thinking it too innocent to harm anyone. The evil god Loki, realising this, fashioned a spear out of mistletoe and put it in the hand of the blind god, Hother. Hother, thinking it a tribute to Balder, threw it at him during a parade, and killed him. All the other gods 'fell a-sighing and a-sobbing', and between them prepared Balder for the grandest funeral ever seen.

The English references – parsons, clerks, mourners and other roles played by various birds – are likely to have been introduced in the 18th century, when the rhyme was used to commemorate the death of Robert Walpole, first prime minister.

WHEN ORNITHOLOGY AND POLITICS DON'T MIX

You know you should stay off the hustings when:

- you think that LBJ was not an American president
- as far as you're concerned, the greatest ever Tory invented the field guide
- the phrase 'philanthropic government' makes you think of a cabinet of small water birds
- you refer to Arthur Scargill as the Red Grouse
- you think you need binoculars on the campaign trail
- you're sure the home secretary is called Jack Snipe
- you're confident the Green Party won't get in at the next election, but they might just squeeze it at the one after that.

JAWS I AND II

All living birds are classified into one of two 'super-orders' based not as might be expected on, say, their ability to fly, or regional distribution, but on their mouths. The Paleognathae, or 'old jaws', are by far the smallest of the two groups, containing just the ratites (ostrich, kiwis, cassowaries and emus) and the tinamous. These birds are grouped together because of their distinctive morphology: their palates are fused and inflexible, whereas those of the Neognathae (new jaws), ie all the other birds, are jointed and flexible.

THE NUTCRACKER'S TREAT

It's a common discovery: you're digging the garden to prepare for the new season, and up with the earth and worms comes an ancient hazelnut on your spade. Yet another squirrel has forgotten where it stored its winter cache.

The Clark's nutcracker of America's Rocky Mountains, however, is not so careless. It buries pine seeds in up to 5,000 different caches through the summer, and research has shown that it's able to find just about all of them nine months later.

The theory behind this remarkable Krypton factor ability is based upon spatial memory. Studies have suggested that although the birds use landmarks, such as trees or rocks, to help them find their buried stores, it's not the distance from those landmarks that is their key, but the compass bearing. By combining a series of bearings from a variety of landmarks, the birds come up with a spatial grid, at each intersection of which lies the buried treasure.

He'd heard other birds talk about it; he wasn't quite sure what it was; but Ozzy Ostrich was damned if he wasn't going to look supercilium too.

WINGED WORDS

The track that I had followed in the evening soon died out, and I continued to follow over a bald turf ascent a row of stone pillars, such as had conducted me across the Goulet. It was already warm. I tied my jacket on the pack, and walked in my knitted waistcoat. Modestine herself was in high spirits, and broke of her own accord, for the first time in my experience, into a jolting trot that set the oats swashing in the pocket of my coat. The view, back upon the northern Gévaudan, extended with every step; scarce a tree, scarce a house, appeared upon the fields of wild hill that ran north, east, and west, all blue and gold in the haze and sunlight of the morning. A multitude of little birds kept sweeping and twittering about my path; they perched on the stone pillars, they pecked and strutted on the turf, and I saw them circle in volleys in the blue air, and show, from time to time, translucent flickering wings between the sun and me.

Robert Louis Stevenson,
Travels with a Donkey in the Cévennes, 1879

100 *Number, in millions, of birds that die each year in the US from flying into glass windows*

THRASHERS AND WARBLERS

Heavy Metal acts are not particularly interested in sparrows, finches or buntings. Or, for that matter, ostriches, penguins or pelicans. They like bold, brooding, swooping species like eagles, crows, and even more eagles and crows. Which means that the name of the last band below was chosen purely to lull listeners into a false sense of security...

The bands:
Crowforce • Eagles Of Death Metal • Falconer
Firebird Band • Hawkwind • Raven • Shrike
Spread Eagle • Birds Of Prey • Budgie

The albums
A Crow Left Of The Murder by Incubus
Lonesome Crow by Scorpions
Turn Loose The Swans by My Dying Bride
The Cuckoo Clocks Of Hell by Buckethead
Swallow This by Poison

Please note: No birds, feathered or metal, were harmed during the compilation of these lists.

QUOTE UNQUOTE

To my father – the first bad birdwatcher I ever met.
He taught me all he knew.
Simon Barnes, writer on birds, from the dedication in
his book *How to be a Bad Birdwatcher*

PLOVER LOVE

Stories from the ornithological world of young birds imprinting on the wrong parents are well documented: Konrad Lorenz and the goslings that loved him; whooping crane specialists who dress in crane costumes while around the chicks to keep them thinking that they're birds.

But occasionally a story comes through of a chick imprinting on its real parents, but in the wrong way. In 1994, Dutch ornithologist Holmer Vonk came across a seven-day-old grey plover chick while studying the birds on the Siberian tundra. It was running around with a pronounced limp. He caught the little bird, and found that its leg was absolutely fine.

Further investigation showed that the mother did in fact have a genuine limp, and that its chick was simply following, so to speak, in her footsteps.

HOW TO CATCH AN EAGLE, CHEYENNE-STYLE

From the observations of E Adamson Hoebel, anthropologist:

Eagles are not eaten but are highly prized for their feathers. They are caught by human hand and strangled. This is a crafty, ticklish undertaking, and one for specialists only – men who have eagle-catching power and knowledge of its associated rituals. Eagles have a wing-spread up to seven feet and a beak as long as their heads.

The trick is done from a pit-blind, which must be painstakingly prepared. The pit can be dug only when there are no eagles in the sky, and the dirt must be scattered a long way off, because eagles are far-sighted and cautious. Before digging the pit, the eagle catcher must sing his sacred eagle songs alone in his lodge all night long. His pit, which is just large enough for him to sit in, is roofed over with long grass through which are left a few spy holes. He deodorises himself in a sweat bath and greases himself all over with eagle-grease paint.

He enters the hole before daybreak, when the eagles cannot see him. Over his head a piece of fresh bait is tied firmly down. When an eagle settles down to tear at the bait, the hunter slowly slips his hands through the grass, grabs its legs and pulls it into the hole. The hunter is then in a 3-by-5 hole with a fighting, clawing eagle that he must strangle with a noose!

The reward is considerable prestige and a good return in trade value: a horse for twenty or thirty feathers, for example. Eagle catching must be done in four-day stints (a ritual requirement). At the end, a ceremonial offering and apology are made to the dead eagles, followed by the hunter's taking four sweat baths to neutralise the sacred power worked up for use in the enterprise.

COLOUR ME AMAZED

Albinism	Lack of pigmentation, causing whiteness
Erythrism	Excessive red pigmentation
Flavism	Excessive yellow pigmentation
Heterochroism	General term for unusual colour change
Leucism	Reduction of pigmentation, causing a washed-out look
Melanism	Excessive melanin pigmentation, causing a sooty look
Schizochroism	Pigmentation is fine, except for one missing colour

BIRDBRAINERS

What am I?
CHAWFH
Answer on page 153

SPECIFIC DETAILS

How many species of bird are there in the world? It all depends on your definition of species. The constant recategorising of subspecies, species, genus and even family means that the total is ever changing. For the record, however, some accepted totals by classifiers at various times during the last half-century or so have been:

8,590	1951	Mayr and Amadon
9,672	1990	Sibley and Monroe
9,702	1993	Sibley and Monroe
9,730	1994	Sibley and Monroe

In short, 'approximately 10,000' is what you want to say when asked by a non-birder. Unless, that is, you want to follow Richard Bowdler Sharpe (1847-1901). Although bowdlerising generally means taking out the rude bits, this Bowdler preferred to put things back in. Not rude bits, but subspecies. He refused to recognise this category, so ended up in the 19th century with a total of 18,939 recorded species. Few really listened to him.

FEELING FRUITY?

Bananaquit
Plum-faced lorikeet
Eastern lemon dove
Antillean mango
Obscure berrypecker
Nectarinia kilimensis (the bronze sunbird)
Tan(a)gerine

And a veritable fruit bowl of a bird: the orange-breasted fruiteater

BIRDS OF A FEATHER FLOCK TOGETHER

The sight of thousands of starlings swooping and billowing together as dusk approaches is both exciting and inspiring. So imagine what the neighbours of a 16-acre Swiss pine forest must have felt during the winter of 1952/3. For several nights, the birds settled down to get close together for warmth. And their numbers? There were a staggering 72 million of them.

Behaviour, anatomy, breeding habits: all useful tools in the traditional taxonomist's identification kit, as they lump together or split apart the species. But the DNA boys are coming up fast in this field, thanks to their barcoding process.

The barcode is a 648-base-pair section of the gene for cytochrome c oxidase I. This particular stretch accumulates small differences as species diverge, allowing DNA taxonomists to distinguish even closely related species with 98% accuracy.

So just what does cytochrome c oxidase do? The importance of the enzyme is its role as a thermodynamic force for oxidative phosphorylation and its ability to contain dangerous partially reduced intermediates, superoxides, which can cause genetic and tissue damage. Located in the inner mitochondrial membrane, the electrons flow through it and are accepted by oxygen. The oxygen which has a high affinity for electrons is reduced to produce water. During this process, protons are pumped outside to the inter-membrane space from the matrix. This proton gradient is used by ATP synthase to produce ATP. Or at least, so says the chemical dictionary.

This piece of trivia is a little more palatable however: cytochrome c oxidase was first isolated in baker's yeast in 1940.

...IS CONNECTED TO THE...

The green sandpiper was known in Norfolk as the martin snipe
The jack snipe was known in Orkney as the plover's page
The grey plover was known in Yorkshire as the sea pigeon
The woodpigeon was known in Yorkshire as the clatter dove
The stock dove was known in Cheshire as the sand pigeon
The green sandpiper was known...

BIRDSVILLE

Longreach, a town in Queensland, Australia, has a unique distinction. All its roads are named after birds. So if you'd like to stay at the Town Lodge, just take a walk up Bustard Street. Or if you're staying at the Caravan Park, then look out for Ibis Street.

If you lose your sense of direction, however, your knowledge of birds will help. Streets named after water birds run east-west, while those named after land birds run north-south.

WINGED WORDS

The yellowhammer is the most persistent individually, but I think the blackbirds when listened to are the masters of the fields. Before one can finish another begins, like the summer ripples succeeding behind each other, so that the melodious sound merely changes its position. Now here, now in the corner, then across the field, again in the distant copse, where it seems about to sink, when it rises again almost at hand. Like a great human artist, the blackbird makes no effort, being fully conscious that his liquid tone cannot be matched. He utters a few delicious notes, and carelessly quits the green stage of the oak till it pleases him to sing again. Without the blackbird, in whose throat the sweetness of the green fields dwells, the days would be only partly summer. Without the violet all the bluebells and cowslips could not make a spring, and without the blackbird, even the nightingale would be but half welcome.

Richard Jefferies,
The Life of the Fields, **1884**

QUOTE UNQUOTE

I don't like small birds. They hop around so merrily outside my window, looking so innocent. But I know that secretly, they're watching my every move and plotting to beat me over the head with a large steel pipe and take my shoe.
Jack Handy, comedian

BORN TO LOVE BIRDS

Otto Finsch (1839–1917) was the aptly named curator of the bird collections at the Rijksmuseum at Leiden, yet in his earlier days he was a much travelled naturalist and explorer. Silesian born (now part of Germany, Poland and Czech Republic), he visited Bulgaria aged just 19 where he worked as a tutor and in his spare time prepared a paper on the country's birds. Joining the zoologist Alfred Brehm on expeditions to Turkestan and China in his late 30s, he picked up a taste for long-distance travel, and packed Polynesia, New Zealand, Australia and New Guinea into his next trip, studying birds all the while. Several species now bear his name.

Outside of ornithology, he's best known for his efforts to make north-eastern New Guinea a German protectorate, which eventually became known as the Bismarck Archipelago, its capital town being named Finschhafen. He also bears the unusual honour of having one of the moon's craters named after him.

BANKING ON BIRDS IN BOTSWANA

Several countries have featured birds on their banknotes, but few have crammed in as many as Botswana. The southern African country, whose currency is the pula, has deposited:

Hoopoe	1 pula note
Grey lourie	2 pula note
Helmeted guineafowl	5 pula note
Monteiro's hornbill	10 pula note
Ostrich	20 pula note
Malachite kingfisher	50 pula note (front)
African fish eagle	50 pula note (back) and 100 pula note

THE GUANO WARS

Whenever any citizen of the United States discovers a deposit of guano on any island, rock, or key, not within the lawful jurisdiction of any other Government, and not occupied by the citizens of any other Government, and takes peaceable possession thereof, and occupies the same, such island, rock, or key may, at the discretion of the President, be considered as appertaining to the United States.

This was the rather remarkable decree of America's 1856 Guano Islands Act, passed at a time when inter-continental rivalry for the precious bird-droppings, that made such a difference to agriculture, had reached an all-time high. Discovering that Peruvian guano was a considerably better fertiliser than their own home-grown stuff, America started to make a move to mine it, but were beaten to the punch by the British, who managed to obtain sole trading rights in the stuff from that country. American farmers, angered by the high premium they were now having to pay, demanded of their government greater guano-gathering opportunities, and the imperialistic Act was passed.

Within just a few years, courts, ambassadors and Congress were protecting the rights of guano-miners in some of the far-flung islands of the Pacific Ocean, as the hunt continued. Eventually, synthetic fertilisers took over from the natural materials, and America was left with a number of rocky possessions scattered through the oceans off its seaboards. They've been put to unusual use, though. During the cold war, it is believed that some of the guano islands were used by the CIA as outposts to listen in on the doings of Cuba and Nicaragua. Today, Baker Island, Jarvis Island, Howland Island, Kingman Reef, Johnston Atoll and Midway Atoll still remain under US control. And they've still got some guano on them.

BIRDBRAINERS

Take a duck, replace a point with a penny, and what do you get?
Answer on page 153

THROUGH WHITE'S EYES

Birds as observed by Gilbert White in his
***Natural History of Selborne*, 1788/9**

On the fifth of July, 1775, I again untiled part of a roof over the nest of a swift. The dam sat in the nest; but so strongly was she affected... for her brood, which she supposed to be in danger, that, regardless of her own safety, she would not stir, but lay sullenly by them, permitting herself to be taken in hand. The squab young we brought down and placed on the grass-plot, where they tumbled about, and were as helpless as a new-born child. While we contemplated their naked bodies, their unwieldy disproportioned abdomina, and their heads, too heavy for their necks to support, we could not but wonder when we reflected that these shiftless beings in a little more than a fortnight would be able to dash through the air almost with the inconceivable swiftness of a meteor; and perhaps, in their emigration must traverse vast continents and oceans as distant as the equator. So soon does nature advance small birds to their state of perfection; while the progressive growth of men and large quadrupeds is slow and tedious!

QUOTE UNQUOTE

My father told me all about the birds and the bees, the liar.
I went steady with a woodpecker till I was 21.
Bob Hope, comedian

THE EARLY BIRDS

In addition to the archaeopteryx, the following lived with the dinosaurs:

Confuciusornis	120 million years old, chicken-sized, toothless beak, claws on wing, found in China
Eoalulavis	115 myo, decent flier, tuft of feathers attached to digit
Sinornis	110 myo, sparrow-sized, teeth, reversed hallux, or main toe
Enantiornithes	80 myo, large group of birds, wing skeleton, many species
Rahona	70 myo, feathered wings, long tail, sickle claw like raptors

Number of fish brought to the nest over 52 days by a male osprey at Rutland 107
Water in 2002

BIRD PROVERBS FROM AROUND THE WORLD

A chattering bird builds no nest.
Cameroon

*A bird does not sing because it
has an answer, but because it
has a song.*
China

*You cannot prevent the birds of
sorrow from flying over your
head, but you can prevent them
from building nests in your hair.*
China

*Two birds disputed about a ker-
nel; a third swooped down and
carried it off.*
Congo

Old birds are hard to pluck.
Germany

A crab does not beget a bird.
Ghana

*No need to teach an
eagle to fly.*
Greece

*Each bird loves to hear
himself sing.*
Italy

*God gives every bird his worm,
but he does not throw it into
the nest.*
Sweden

REMEMBERING THE PORTUGUESE

Would you rather be Vasco da Gama or Ferdinand Magellan? Here's
some advice: if penguins are your bird, plump for the latter. The
two explorers commanded the first western expeditions to describe
penguins, discovering two species in particular. Magellan's bird is
now known as the Magellanic penguin, which is very nice for him.
Honoured by history, and all that. Vasco da Gama did not do so
well. His species? The jackass penguin.

WINGED WORDS

I saw the white gulls hovering around the great granite rocks of our
Land's End and admiring their wives, who were detained at home
on urgent private affairs, and for once in an excursive life was
allowed to enjoy an interesting view without that chattering
abomination called a guide. No one bored me with statements
which I knew as well as he; no one came to explain the difference
between a kittiwake and a scissor-bill and expected a shilling; no
one pressed me to purchase blurred, grimy, thirty-second-rate
photographs, conchological specimens, or lemonade. I turned my
face from the kittiwakes towards home.

S Reynolds Hole, Dean of Rochester,
A Book about the Garden, 1892

'Why not break the bond and be single, take a fierce stoop and a swing back, as when a gannet plunges like a white, metallic arrow into the sea, raising a burst of spray, disappearing, completing the downward curve of the parabola in the invisible underwater where it seizes the object of desire, then away, away with success upwards, back flashing into the air and white space?'

So asks DH Lawrence of love, in his book *Kangaroo*. But there is a more pragmatic gannet question that this extract raises. Why don't they break their necks every time they dive?

Gannets scan the seas from heights of up to 30 metres, thrusting into the waters like daggers once they've spotted their prey, sending up a spray of water that can leap up to three metres high. The bird's momentum carries it well below the surface, sometimes even below its prey, which it catches on the way back up. In order to absorb the impact of the plunge, it inflates air cells under the skin at the last moment which, like an air bag in a car, cushion the blow. Closely fitting bills and no external nostril openings keep water out of its head, while the lower bill is fitted with thick plates that further protect it from impact.

Like birds of prey, the gannet also has eyes towards the front of its head, giving it binocular vision for the underwater chase.

TOO TALL TO FLY

Ostrich	9 ft
Emu	6 ft 2 in
Cassowary	5 ft 6 in
Rhea	4 ft 6 in
Emperor Penguin	3 ft 10 in

GARDENERS ARE PIGS

Robins, confident hoppers around our feet as we dig up our back garden potatoes, are much shyer creatures on the Continent. Why should this be? The thinking is that the bird became used in centuries past to the British abundance of wild boar in the ancient woodland, and would follow the huge pigs around for pickings after they'd snuffled up the ground. Once the boar became extinct, the robin simply turned its attention to the efforts of another large grunting mammal, the ubiquitous British gardener.

BIRDBRAINERS

Chopping out two-thirds of a website (5 letters)

Answer on page 153

ABSOLUTELY FABULOUS

The Vain Jackdaw, by Aesop

Jupiter announced that he intended to appoint a king over the birds, and named a day on which they were to appear before his throne, when he would select the most beautiful of them all to be their ruler. Wishing to look their best on the occasion they repaired to the banks of a stream, where they busied themselves in washing and preening their feathers. The Jackdaw was there along with the rest, and realised that, with his ugly plumage, he would have no chance of being chosen as he was: so he waited till they were all gone, and then picked up the most gaudy of the feathers they had dropped, and fastened them about his own body, with the result that he looked gayer than any of them. When the appointed day came, the birds assembled before Jupiter's throne. After passing them in review, he was about to make the Jackdaw king, when all the rest set upon the king-select, stripped him of his borrowed plumes, and exposed him for the Jackdaw that he was.

It is not only fine feathers that make fine birds.

Guidelines as laid down by UK Zoo Standards Review, 1999, and followed by WWT.

Non-domestic waterfowl must always be kept in an exhibit which is fox-proof, without the need to shut them in to a house or shed overnight. This does not apply to domesticated waterfowl types, where this practice is widespread and acceptable.

Pairs of swans, some goose and duck species, sometimes individual birds, may need to be kept separately, due to incompatibility with birds of the same species and/or birds of other species. Provision for this should be made at all times.

Swans and geese and some species of duck need access to grass for food. Supplementary feeding, in the form of pellets can be a substitute in the winter months, when grass levels are low. The stocking density and types of birds in any pen should reflect the fact that grass will need to re-establish itself in the spring.

As a general rule, ducks, swans and flamingos need water to drink, bathe, breed, swim and live. Water should ideally be flowing at all times, with fresh supplies for topping up or through flow available. Pens should be at least 50% water to land, although this can vary with flamingos needing much more of a wet pen with substantial, but not exclusively, areas of shallow water. As a general rule, geese need water to drink, bathe and breed, and a greater need for grass. Therefore a pen that is 20% water to land is acceptable, although in a bigger enclosure where there is sufficient land available, a larger water area is preferred. Flamingos will need a small area of deeper water (one metre) where they can swim and copulate. Diving duck species require at least 50% of their water area to be at least 600mm and ideally one metre in depth.

All birds should ideally be able to get out of a water body wherever they choose. Therefore edges should be sloping, with the gradient no steeper than 30 degrees. It is often acceptable to have ramps in place where this is not possible however, but this is not ideal especially with diving duck spp.

Size of enclosure and carrying capacity. This can be complicated as many birds are kept in small or even large flocks. As a general guideline a minimum size for a pair of birds in the following categories would be as follows:

- small duck, (teal, smew) - 50 m2
- large duck, (yellowbill, shelduck) – 100 m2
- small goose, (orinoco, redbreasted) – 200 m2
- large goose, (cereopsis, pinkfoot) – 300 m2
- swan, (trumpeter, Bewick's) – 400 m2
- flamingo group of 10 birds – 400 m2.

When the pelican has gorged its stomach with fish, it often flies off into the desert, and there remains alone until it has digested its food. This, and this only, must be the allusion of the psalmist: 'I am like a pelican of the wilderness,' all alone. By the river side I have seen thousands of pelicans, standing in files, like regiments of soldiers.

...The Arabs have various ways of catching partridges; one of which is with nets; and they will sometimes place a few tame ones in a cage in the net to entice the wild ones. This, doubtless, is the 'snare of the fowler' referred to in Psalms xci 3; Prov vi 5. How subtle the enemy is! He can employ tame birds, or singing birds, or any other kind of birds, to catch his prey, when and as it suits his purpose.

John Gadsby, *Wanderings in the East*, 1860.

Gadsby, a deeply religious soul, spent several years in the mid-19th century travelling around the Middle East, meticulously recording his observations, in an attempt to discover the origin of as many Biblical references as he could.

QUOTE UNQUOTE

There is nothing in which the birds differ more from man than the way in which they can build and yet leave a landscape as it was before.
Robert Lynd, essayist

LAURENCE OF MALAYSIA

Although some dispute the claim, Laurence Poh was probably the man who introduced one of the great revolutions of modern birdwatching: digiscoping.

Like so many inventions that seem so obvious in retrospect, digiscoping (the actual term itself was coined by Alain Fosse) was born of necessity. Unable to identify a raptor on a distant tree in his beloved Malaysia, Poh desperately turned to his new digital camera. Holding it up to the eyepiece of his telescope, he took the shot and crossed his fingers. It worked.

Today, digiscoping has gone through the roof. Manufacturers provide two-in-one pieces of equipment, complete with attachments to hold the camera steady, and many an identification is made from previously unobtainable photographic evidence.

But the technique will have to continue to grow without Laurence. The 'Father of Digiscoping' died peacefully in his sleep of pancreatic cancer in September 2004.

F-OWL PLAY

The flammulated owl of the oak forests of the western US is almost entirely insectivorous... but occasionally bites off more than it can chew. In 1947 a researcher examined the stomach contents of a dead individual he had found, and found four crane flies, one caddisfly, seven moths, 11 harvestmen, and one long-horned grasshopper.

This last was the mistake. The bird had choked to death on it.

MEANWHILE, BRINGING UP THE REAR

Arsefoot	Old southern name for great crested grebe
Bitter bum	Old southern name for bittern
Bum towel	Old Devonian name for long-tailed tit
Shite scouter	Old Scottish name for Arctic skua
White ass	Old Cornish name for wheatear

NB: the skua got its name from the belief that it chased gulls until they dropped excrement, which the bird then devoured.

THE STORIES BEHIND THE BIRDS OF HOLLYWOOD

'So, what're we gonna do?' 'I dunno, what d'ya wanna do?' The vultures who appeared at the end of Disney's *The Jungle Book*, with their London and Liverpool accents, lived dull lives brightened only by the brief appearance of Mowgli and his adventures. The actors behind the voices did a little bit more, however. So, what did they do?

J Pat O'Malley (Buzzie), who also voiced Colonel Hathi, was a staple Disney character voice, putting the words to the Colonel and Jasper in *101 Dalmatians*, the Walrus in *Alice in Wonderland*, and Cyril Proudbottom in *The Adventures of Ichabod and Mr Toad*. He made many TV appearances, too, from *Taxi* to *Fantasy Island*, and *The Rockford Files* to *Batman*.

Lord Tim Hudson (Dizzy) cropped up again in *The Aristocats* voicing English Cat. He was a music producer, and a DJ on KFWB, who went on to become the manager of English cricketer Ian Botham.

Digby Wolfe (Ziggy) won an Emmy award in 1968 for his writing on *Rowan and Martin's Laugh-in*. He also wrote for Goldie Hawn.

Chad Stuart (Flaps) was the first half of the 60s singing duo Chad and Jeremy. His real name is Stuart Chadwick. He also appeared in *Batman*.

Originally writing it as a musical light entertainment in 1886, Camille Saint-Saens only allowed the *Carnival of the Animals* to be played twice during his lifetime, as he feared it might damage his reputation as a serious musician. In one sense, he was right: the 22-minute piece, which in its 14 segments depicts a parade of beasts, birds and buffoons, is the work for which he is popularly best remembered today.

Yet the *Carnival* contains much to admire. The Swan, for example, has become the cello's cornerstone piece, taught to young cellists to demonstrate the soulful range and grace of the instrument, while the haunting nature of the cuckoo, played by the clarinet in an orchestral wood, should be listened to by all birdwatchers. It perfectly sums up the pleasure of wandering hopefully between the trees as a bird call echoes out in the distance.

Frantic hens and cocks, and a busy aviary are the remaining feathered items in the *Carnival*, although elephants, tortoises, lions, kangaroos and more also rumble and tumble through. The piece is full of gags, too, as works by Berlioz, Offenbach and even Saint-Saens himself are remastered for the musical jape.

But perhaps the main point of the piece is buried in the middle as section 8. Personages with Long Ears was Saint-Saens' jab at asinine music critics as they pompously hee-haw their comments about his work. The message is clear, even over a century after it was written. Despite his worries about how it would be perceived, you should condemn *Carnival of the Animals* at your peril: Saint-Saens is laughing right back at you.

FEATHERS OF A BIRD

Contour and down feathers are those that we're all familiar with, giving as they do the shape, form, flying ability and fluffiness of a bird. Yet there are four other types too:

- **Semiplumes:** halfway between contour and down, helping to supply insulation and a certain amount of shape to the bird.
- **Filoplumes:** only a few barbs at the tips; these feathers probably provide a sensory function, helping birds to keep their feathers in order.
- **Bristles:** stiff, protective feathers around the eyes and mouth of some species.
- **Powder feathers:** these feathers continue to grow through adulthood, disintegrating at the end and creating a fine powder that helps keep plumage clean.

THE STORIES BEHIND THE
BIRDS OF HOLLYWOOD

When Cameron Diaz identifies a bird call as that of a pygmy nuthatch, only found in Carmel, California, then she and Charlie's other Angels in the 2000 movie have their key clue as to the whereabouts of the baddie. Ornithology wins the day.

Except it doesn't. The call is not of any nuthatch at all, but a warbler, and when we see the bird, it's actually a troupial, which bears no resemblance whatsoever, and is actually South American. So, wrong bird, and wrong call. Finally, the pygmy nuthatch isn't endemic to Carmel at all, but found all over the western states. In short, a complete nonsense.

Now that's putting the charlie into *Charlie's Angels*.

ACTS OF GODWITS

Knud Rasmussen, explorer and ethnologist, died of food poisoning from eating bad dovekies (little auks) in 1933.

Lt Cal Rogers in 1912 was the first airman to be killed by a bird strike, when a gull became entangled in his flight controls while flying over Long Beach, California.

In 2002, a pensioner collapsed and died of a heart attack in his Anglesey garden following an attack from dive-bombing herring gulls.

There are eight records of people being kicked to death by an ostrich.

In the 1920s, a young boy was killed by a cassowary in Australia, after it had been attacked by his dog.

In 1859, Sitting Bull's father was killed by a Crow. Warrior, that is.

WINGED WORDS

The nightingale shows no timidity while all is still, but sings on the bough in full sight, hardly three yards away, so that you can see the throat swell as the notes are poured forth – now in intricate trills, now a low, sweet call, then a liquid 'jug-jug-jug!' To me it sounds richer in the morning – sunlight, flowers, and the rustle of green leaves seem the natural accompaniment; and the distant chorus of other birds affords a contrast and relief – an orchestra filling up the pauses and supporting the solo singer.

Richard Jefferies, *Wild Life in a Southern County*, 1879

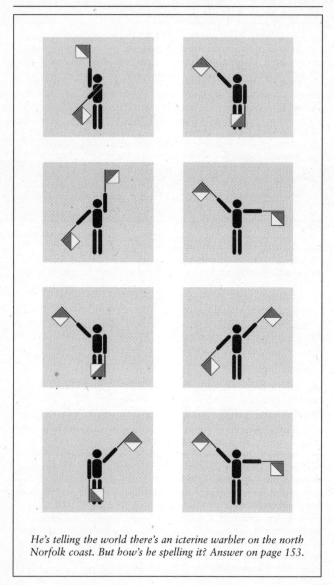

He's telling the world there's an icterine warbler on the north Norfolk coast. But how's he spelling it? Answer on page 153.

Varieties of four-toed avian feet

Foot type	Description	Example
Anisodactyl	Hallux is behind, other three toes are in front.	Blackbird
Syndactyl	The third and fourth toes are united for most of their length	Kingfisher
Zygodactyl	Second and third toes in front, fourth and hallux behind	Woodpecker
Heterodactyl	Like zygodactyl foot except the inner toe is reversed	Trogon
Raptorial	Toes deeply cleft, with large, strong, sharply curved talons	Raptor
Semipalmate	Anterior toes joined part way by a small webbing	Semipalmated Plover
Totipalmate	All four toes united by large webs	Cormorant
Palmate	Front toes united	Mallard
Lobate	Swimming foot with a series of lateral lobes on the toes	Grebe

The hallux is the big, or main toe

PUFFIN ON THE MENU

Who'd be a North Sea seabird today? Not only have sandeel stocks been heavily depleted by fishing, but many of those that remain have moved further north to follow the plankton that have been taking advantage of the globally warming Arctic Circle. Fewer sandeels mean less successful breeding seasons, and 2004 was a complete disaster for the birds of Shetland and Orkney in particular, many colonies producing not a single surviving chick between them.

And now they've got a new threat, and it comes from their own order. The great skua, or bonxie, a true pirate of the seas, is also struggling with the changing fish stocks, and changing its diet. It's eating far more birds than before. Fulmars, puffins, guillemots, razorbills and storm petrels are all turning up on the menu, which added to the recent breeding disaster could help tip some species into severe decline.

In short, global warming is encouraging birds to eat each other at an unhealthy rate. And still governments scratch their heads and wonder.

SOMETHING TO GROUSE
ABOUT IN SCOTLAND

In 2004, *The Scotsman* ran a poll to discover the national bird of Scotland. Although the golden eagle soared away with the final victory, an astonishing late surge – some 1,200 votes – by the red grouse raised a few eyebrows at polling headquarters. After a quick investigation, it turned out that the good people of Famous Grouse whisky had emailed their main customers to suggest they vote for their well-known emblem.

The cheeky shenanigans were rooted out, and the final results stood as follows:

1. Golden eagle
2. Red grouse
3. Capercaillie
4. Osprey
5. Puffin
6. Gannet
7. Sea eagle
8. Peregrine
9. Crested tit
10. Lapwing
11. Scottish crossbill
12. Ptarmigan

QUOTE UNQUOTE

Birds sing after a storm. Why shouldn't we?
Rose Fitzgerald Kennedy, presidential matriarch

IN DECLINE, BUT SHOOT IT ANYWAY

Is it possible for a bird to be on the Red List as a bird of conservation concern, yet be one of only a handful that it is still legal to kill under general licence? Bizarrely, until January 2005, the house sparrow and starling both shared that fate.

A few years ago each species was so common that they were viewed as cullable if they were causing damage to crops or spreading disease. That was before their populations went into freefall, the house sparrow in particular halving in numbers in just a few years. They were quickly put onto the Red List once their severe decline was noticed, but it took a further two years before they were given the full protection that almost all other British species receive.

WHAT'S IN A NAME?

The poor old dotterel, he just doesn't get any respect. Thanks to the male's habit of squatting tight on its nest and allowing any old soul to just wander right up to him, the bird was viewed as stupid by early observers, who gave it its name which comes from the same root as dotard and dotty... the stupid one. To add insult to injury, however, science joined in. The bird's specific name, *(Charadrius) morinellus*, means 'little fool'. In Gaelic, meanwhile, it's called An Tamadan Mointich – peat-bog fool.

WINGED WORDS

'Ah!' said Tim, 'you look tired though, now I come to look at you. Hark! there he is, d'ye hear him? That was Dick, the blackbird. He hasn't been himself since you've been gone. He'd never get on without you, now; he takes as naturally to you as he does to me.'

'Dick is a far less sagacious fellow than I supposed him, if he thinks I am half so well worthy of his notice as you,' replied Nicholas.

'Why, I'll tell you what, sir,' said Tim, standing in his favourite attitude and pointing to the cage with the feather of his pen, 'it's a very extraordinary thing about that bird, that the only people he ever takes the smallest notice of, are Mr Charles, and Mr Ned, and you, and me.'

Here, Tim stopped and glanced anxiously at Nicholas; then unexpectedly catching his eye repeated, 'And you and me, sir, and you and me.'

Charles Dickens, *Nicholas Nickleby*, 1838/9

10 BIRDS BEGINNING WITH Z

Zamboanga bulbul
Zanzibar bishop
Zapata rail
Zebra finch
Zenaida dove
Zenker's honeyguide
Zimmer's tody-tyrant
Zino's petrel
Zitting cisticola
Zone-tailed hawk
Plus: the Zigzag heron, which doubles its Zedness
with its scientific name *Zebrilus undulatus*.

BIRDBRAINERS

What kind of finch am I?
LLBI
Answer on page 153

ABSOLUTELY FABULOUS

The Crow and the Raven, by Aesop

A crow was jealous of the raven, because he was considered a bird of good omen and always attracted the attention of men, who noted by his flight the good or evil course of future events. Seeing some travellers approaching, the crow flew up into a tree, and perching herself on one of the branches, cawed as loudly as she could. The travellers turned towards the sound and wondered what it foreboded, when one of them laughed and said to his companion: 'Let us proceed on our journey, my friend, for it is only the caw of a crow, and her cry, you know, is no omen.'

Those who assume a character which does not belong to them, only make themselves ridiculous.

QUOTE UNQUOTE

*A very cold morning – hail and snow showers all day… we…
walked backwards and forwards in Brothers wood. William tired
himself with seeking an epithet for the cuckoo.*
Dorothy Wordsworth, May 14 1802

LET'S TALK MAORI

Blue duck	whio
Brown teal	pateke
Dabchick	weweia
Fantail	piwakawaka
Godwit	kuaka
Kingfisher	kotare
Little blue penguin	korora
Little shag	kawaupaka
New Zealand shoveler	kuruwhengi
Pied stilt	poaka
Rifleman	titipounamu
Robin	toutouwai
Stitchbird	hihi
Takahe	take a guess

The Wildfowl & Wetlands Trust has nine sites in the UK, covering between them over 4000 acres. Here's how to find them.

WWT Arundel
The Wildfowl & Wetlands Trust
Mill Street, Arundel
West Sussex
BN18 9PB UK
T: 01903 883355
F: 01903 884834
E: info.arundel@wwt.org.uk
Close to the A27 & A29. On approaching Arundel by road, visitors should follow the brown duck signs. By foot from Arundel railway station, it is half a mile to Arundel Town and a further, gentle mile along Mill Road to the Trust. By Bus, there is a 30-minute service both from Chichester & the West (Route 55), and Brighton, Worthing & the East (Route 702) every weekday to the Arundel Town centre with the same walk along Mill Road.

WWT Caerlaverock
Eastpark Farm, Caerlaverock
Dumfriesshire, Scotland
DG1 4RS
T: 01387 770200
F: 01387 770539
E: info.caerlaverock@wwt.org.uk
9 miles south east of Dumfries. Follow tourist signs from A75 west of Annan or St. Michael's church in Dumfries. Nearest railway and coach stations Dumfries; limited bus service to Caerlaverock.

WWT Castle Espie
Ballydrain Road, Comber,
County Down
BT23 6EA
T: 0289 1874146
F: 0289 1873857
E: info.castleespie@wwt.org.uk
Located on Strangford Lough, 3 miles south of Comber and 13 miles south-east of Belfast. Signposted from the A22 Comber-Killyleagh-Downpatrick road.

London Wetland Centre
The Wildfowl & Wetlands Trust
Queen Elizabeth's Walk
Barnes, London SW13 9WT
T: 020 8409 4400
E: info.london@wwt.org.uk
The London Wetland Centre is easily accessible by car, situated less than one mile from the South Circular (A205) at Roehampton and the A4 at Hammersmith. There is ample parking available at the Centre. Most major routes join the North Circular (A406). Travel south along the A406 to the junction with the A4 at Brentford (the M4 becomes the A4 at this point). Head east along the A4 before taking the A306 south across Hammersmith Bridge to Barnes where you will pick up the signs for the London Wetland Centre. Turn left at the Red Lion pub into Queen Elizabeth Walk. The main entrance is 300 metres on the left. If coming from the South East, in South London take the South Circular (A205). Leave the A205 at Roehampton, taking the A306 towards Barnes before picking up the signs for the London Wetland Centre. In the SE take the M25, exit at junction

10 and travel north on A3. After the Robin Hood roundabout and Putney Vale exit turn left on to Roehampton Lane (A306), go straight across at the South Circular traffic lights and past Barnes railway station. In Barnes turn right at the Red Lion pub into Queen Elizabeth Walk. The main entrance is 300 metres on the left.

Nearest Underground: Hammersmith Tube. From Hammersmith Tube take the 283, the specially branded Duck Bus, which will bring you directly into the Centre. Alternatively, buses 33, 72 and 209 stop nearby (alight at the Red Lion Pub). From Barnes mainline station take bus 33 or 72 or from Barnes Bridge take bus 209. By train, come from Waterloo, Clapham Junction or Richmond to Barnes or Barnes Bridge. The London Wetland Centre is ten minutes' walk from Barnes station and buses are frequent.

National Wetlands Centre Wales
Llanelli Centre, Penclacwydd, Llwynhendy
Llanelli. SA14 9SH
T: 01554 741087
F: 01554 744101
E: info.llanelli@wwt.org.uk
Situated 1 mile east of Llanelli and 5 miles north west of Swansea. The Centre lies on the eastern side of Carmarthen Bay facing the Gower Peninsula. To find the Centre follow the duck signs off the M4 exiting at junction 47 or 48 we are 1 mile east of Llanelli off the A484 to Swansea. Nearest railway station is Llanelli, bus routes run regularly from Llanelli to Llwynhendy a short walk, bicy-

cle or taxi journey away. The Centre is also on Celtic Trail Route 4.

WWT Martin Mere
The Wildfowl & Wetlands Trust
Burscough, Lancashire, L40 0TA
T: 01704 895181
F: 01704 892343
E: info.martinmere@wwt.org.uk
Located 6 miles from Ormskirk and 10 miles from Southport, situated off the A59, it is signposted from the M61, M58 and M6. There is a no.3 bus service from Ormskirk (except Sundays). Burscough railway station (on the Southport – Manchester line) is approximately one mile from WWT Martin Mere. Cyclists are always welcome.

WWT Slimbridge
The Wildfowl & Wetlands Trust
Slimbridge, Gloucestershire GL2 7BT
T: 0870 334 4000
F: 01453 890827
E: info.slimbridge@wwt.org.uk
Located between Bristol and Gloucester. Follow the signs from M5 (junction 13 or 14). Nearest railway station is Cam/Dursley – a short bicycle or taxi journey away. Also on Sustrans route 41. Sunday bus service from Gloucester. Train/bus 24hr info line: 01452 425543.

WWT Washington
The Wildfowl & Wetlands Trust
District 15, Washington, Tyne and Wear
NE38 8LE
T: 0191 416 5454
F: 0191 416 5801
E: info.washington@wwt.org.uk
Located east of Washington in

District 15, four miles from A1(M), one mile from A19. Signposted off A195, A19, A182 and A1231. By bus: WWT Washington is served by buses to Waterview Park. Direct services are available from Newcastle, Sunderland, Durham, South Shields and Washington town centre. WWT Washington is a 200m walk from Waterview Park. Contact Traveline North East for timetable and fare details 0870 608 2608. By bike: River Wear trail passes the Centre as does the C2C cycle route. Cycle racks provided.

WWT Welney
The Wildfowl & Wetlands Trust
Hundred Foot Bank, Welney
Wisbech
PE14 9TN
T: 01353 860711
F: 01353 860711
E: info.welney@wwt.org.uk
Located 12 miles north of Ely, 26 miles north of Cambridge and 33 miles east of Peterborough.

WHAT'S IN A NAME?

So which is it to be, flax, thistle or hemp? Its names suggest that the linnet goes for the seeds of all three. 'Linnet', like 'linen', comes from the Latin for flax, linum, while the bird's generic name, *Carduelis*, derives from carduus, or thistle. Its scientific moniker *cannabina* however, puts its suggested foodstuff on an altogether more adventurous list.

But then seed eating is what the linnet is all about; like the twite, it even feeds them, particularly those from oilseed rape, to its young.

AN EGGSACT SCIENCE?

Since the beginning of space flight there have been about 200 explosions in space, each sending fragments of debris into orbit around the earth. With nearly 10,000 pieces of space junk over 10cm long already being tracked, and goodness knows how many smaller items also being out there, the threat to satellites has long concerned global space agencies. A new theory is currently being tested, however, that might help scientists track the smaller items. And it all comes down to the egg.

It seems that eggshells and rocket casings explode in similar fashions. Each breaks up according to a power law that results in lots of small and medium-sized pieces and a few larger ones. By repeated exploding of eggshells, the European Space Agency is developing a model to help predict the size and number of fragments of space debris, depending on the nature of an explosion.

A serious case of going to work on an egg.

Bombay duck, well known for not being wildfowl at all, is of course the name given to the dried marine lizardfish that is occasionally found on Indian menus, tight EC regulations permitting, in Europe. But how did it get its name in the first place?

The theory is that 19th century Europeans who were embarking on their rampant colonisation of India, found that the smell of the fish as they hung out to dry reminded them of the musty smell of the Bombay mail train, which used to reek up a storm in the monsoon season. 'Dak' is Hindi for mail, so the Bombay Dak came into being.

The reason they didn't use the Hindi term for the dish was because 'bummalo' sounded a little too crude to the sensitive colonial ear. All very well, but ditching bummalo in favour of a bird name from the family Anas, seems in retrospect a little out of the frying pan...

GREENBACKED H(M)ONEYGUIDE

Dollarbird:	An eastern species of roller named for its coin-sized white wing-tip patches
Dormilon lira:	Spanish for the lyre-tailed nightjar
Escudo hummingbird:	This species lives only on Escudo de Veraguas Island off the Caribbean coast of Panama
Rand's Warbler:	Named after an American 20th century ornithologist
Two-penny chick:	Alternative name for the yellow-breasted crake
Predecimalised birds :	Guineafowl, bobwhite quail, crowned eagle and copper sunbird

WINGED WORDS

Showing that every generation hankers for the bird-rich countryside of 50 years ago.

From end to end of the level landscape came notes of stock-dove and field lark, whilst every coppice rang with chirps and pipings, and around every wayside pool flashed kingfishers, wagtail and yellow hammer. Rural England of fifty years agone yet remained a bird-haunted, bird-beautiful land. In lane and spinney folks listened to woodland singers, instead of identifying them in that mausoleum of animal life, the Natural History Museum.

M Betham-Edwards, *The Lord of the Harvest*, 1899

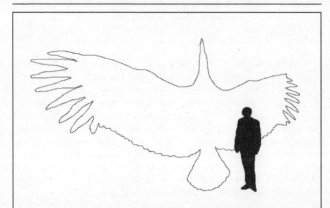

The teratorns, the largest birds ever to fly, lived in what is now California during the Miocene period at least 5 million years ago and were, unsurprisingly, relatives of the condors. Yet what is truly surprising was their size: these mighty meat-eaters included among their number *Teratornis incredibilis*, whose wingspan measured approximately 16.5 feet (the California condor reaches a mere 9.5 feet).

Yet even the incredible incredibilis might have met its match. Another relative from further south was *Argentavis magnificens*, (above) an extraordinary beast. Although some believe its size rendered it incapable of flight (it was at least 5 feet tall), its fossils have revealed slight impressions of feathers – some 5 feet long! – which keep the jury out.

If it could have taken to the air, it would have made an impressive sight. Its wingspan would have been 25 feet wide!

IT'S THE WAY YOU SAY IT

Looks like	Pronounced (according to OED)
Hoopoe	hu-pu
Capercaillie	capper-caylee
Pochard	poe-shud
Scaup	scorp
Oriole	or-eeole
Grouse	vic-tor-mel-droo

BIRDBRAINERS

What am I? An EEsy one
EEEE*E*
Answer on page 153

STEAM-POWERED FLIGHT

What's the difference between the flying steamer duck and the flightless steamer duck? OK, the answer's obvious, but here's the reason why. The flight and tail feathers of the former are a little bit longer than those of its fellow Chilean species, as shown below, giving it the facility of flight, even though it uses it rarely.

Incidentally, the steamer part of the birds' names comes from their habit of paddling rapidly across the water.

	Flying	Flightless
Male wings (mm)	300	275
Female wings (mm)	285	275
Male tail (mm)	107	94
Female tail (mm)	99	88

QUOTE UNQUOTE

Starlings in vast flights drove along like smoke... glimmering and shivering, dim and shadowy, now thickening, deepening, blackening.
S T Coleridge, poet, 27 November 1799

ONE SWALLOW DOES A SPECIES MAKE

The discovery of a new species induces great feeling within the birding world – but occasionally those feelings can be mixed. In May 1984, near Sanganeb lighthouse off Port Sudan, the corpse was found of a swallow that had never before been recorded. Similar to the cliff swallow species, questions were soon asked about where it came from – perhaps Sudan or Eritrea? – and which type of habitat it preferred – probably mountainous. Twenty years on, those questions remain unanswered, as the species, known as the Red Sea swallow, has not been positively identified since.

The bird was given the poignant scientific name of *Hirundo perdita*: the lost swallow.

WINGED WORDS

I caught this morning morning's minion, kingdom of daylight's dauphin,
Dapple-dawn-drawn Falcon, in his riding
Of the rolling level underneath him steady air, and striding
High there, how he rung upon the rein of a wimpling wing
In his ecstasy! then off, off forth on swing,
As a skate's heel sweeps smooth on a bow-bend: the hurl and gliding
Rebuffed the big wind. My heart in hiding
Stirred for a bird, – the achieve of, the mastery of the thing!

Brute beauty and valour and act, oh, air, pride, plume, here
Buckle! AND the fire that breaks from thee then, a billion
Times told lovelier, more dangerous, O my chevalier!

No wonder of it: sheer plod makes plough down sillion
Shine, and blue-bleak embers, ah my dear,
Fall, gall themselves, and gash gold-vermilion.

Gerard Manley Hopkins (1844-1889),
***The Windhover*, published posthumously in 1918**

KEEP ONE IN THE KITCHEN

Ovenbird
Spice finch
Fork-tailed swift
Plate-billed mountain toucan
Spoonbill
Nutcracker
Stock dove

ABSOLUTELY FABULOUS

The Swallow and the Other Birds, by Aesop

It happened that a countryman was sowing some hemp seeds in a field where a Swallow and some other birds were hopping about picking up their food. 'Beware of that man,' quoth the Swallow. 'Why, what is he doing?' said the others. 'That is hemp seed he is sowing; be careful to pick up every one of the seeds, or else you will repent it.' The birds paid no heed to the Swallow's words, and by and by the hemp grew up and was made into cord, and of the cords nets were made, and many a bird that had despised the Swallow's advice was caught in nets made out of that very hemp.

Destroy the seed of evil, or it will grow up to your ruin.

NOW SHOWING AT YOUR LOCAL ORNITHEATRE

The Navy Lark (1959)
Ghost Diver (1957)
Batman & Robin (1997)
Hudson Hawk (1991)
The Eagle has Landed (1976)
Grey Owl (1999)
The Rail Rider (1916)
Higher than a Kite (1943)
And two for the price of one:
The Rookie Cop, aka *Swift Vengeance* (1939)

THE DAY THE WWT GOT LICKED

To commemorate the 50th anniversary of The Wildfowl and Wetlands Trust in 1996, the post office released a special set of Royal Mail stamps, featuring paintings and sketches by the renowned bird artist Charles Tunnicliffe. The heroes chosen to represent their kind were:

19p: Muscovy duckling
25p: Lapwing
30p: White-fronted goose
35p: Bittern
41p: Whooper swan

The choice of the white-fronted goose was particularly poignant. It was seeing these geese that helped Sir Peter Scott found the WWT in the first place, commenting: 'A flock of migrating swans and geese is the last great wildlife spectacle in Britain'.

RESIDENTS OF THE WHITE AVIARY

- Lincoln's sparrow (these birds are known for the stoutness of their bills)
- Washington eagle (a subspecies of the bald eagle)
- *Pycnonotus melanicterus johnsoni* (subspecies of black-crested bulbul, a bird that can be found making a lot of noise in Vietnam)
- *Cardinalis cardinalis clintoni* (a bright and showy subspecies of the cardinal)
- Carter's mollymawk (another name for an albatross, the yellow-nosed species)
- Francolin D Roosevelt
- Aberrant bush warbler (says it all, really)

WINGED WORDS

Between Somerford and Ocksey I saw, on the side of the road, more goldfinches than I had ever seen together; I think fifty times as many as I had ever seen at one time in my life. The favourite food of the goldfinch is the seed of the thistle. This seed is just now dead ripe. The thistles are all cut and carried away from the fields by the harvest; but they grow alongside the roads; and, in this place, in great quantities. So that the goldfinches were got here in flocks, and, as they continued to fly along before me, for nearly half a mile, and still sticking to the road and the banks, I do believe I had, at last, a flock of ten thousand flying before me.

William Cobbett, *Rural Rides*, 1826

A STEP DOWN FROM LITTLE AND LESSER

Dwarf cassowary
Least bittern
Miniature tit-babbler
Pygmy owl
Tiny tyrant manikin
Weebill
And the titchiest name of them all: small minivet

QUOTE UNQUOTE

The soul is a bird, which Satan tries to catch.
A hunchbacked tramp, overheard and
recorded by Maxim Gorky, socialist

DO THE KATUKATUK

**How to re-enact the prairie chicken dance
of the native peoples of Dakota.**

The older women sit on the north side of the room, while the younger women make a circle in the centre of the dancing area. The dance leader then moves into the circle, strutting and dancing while the women move up and down clucking like a female chicken. Then the leader moves back out of the circle to the older women, while making a gutteral sound. He then returns to the circle, then back out again to the men. The next man repeats the process, until each has taken his turn. To finish, the dance leader and one other male dancer return to the circle, and dance themselves into a frenzy, shaking their heads, stamping their feet, and jumping up against each other in mock battle.

One day I paid a visit to Maidenhead, a pleasant town on the Thames, where the Thames is most beautiful, set in the midst of a rich and diversified country which should be a birds' paradise. In my walks in the town, I saw a great many stuffed kingfishers, and, in the shops of the local taxidermists, some rare and beautiful birds, with others that are fast becoming rare. But outside of the town I saw no kingfishers and no rare species at all, and comparatively few birds of any kind. It might have been a town of Philistine cockneys who at no very distant period had emigrated thither from the parish of St Giles-in-the-Fields. I came home with the local guidebook in my pocket. It is now before me, and this is what its writer says of the Thicket, the extensive and beautiful common two miles from the town, which belongs to Maidenhead, or, in other words, to its inhabitants: 'The Thicket was formerly much infested by robbers and highwaymen. The only remains of them to be found now are the snarers of the little feathered songsters, who imprison them in tiny cages and carry them off in large numbers to brighten by their sweet sad sighs for liberty the dwellers in our smoky cities.'

...Will any person maintain for a moment that the eight or nine thousand inhabitants of Maidenhead, and the hundreds or thousands inhabiting the surrounding country could not protect their song-birds from these few men, most of them out of London slums, if they wished or had the spirit to do so?

WH Hudson,
Birds in a Village, 1898

EGGSTRA BIG FOR THE KIWI

- The kiwi's egg is about six times the size it should be for a bird of its size, leading to speculation that the kiwi was once a much larger bird.

- The eggs contain 65% yolk, the largest proportion for any bird (40% is about average), which the newly hatched chick can feed on for a week.

- It takes the female 30 days to form her egg, which makes up 20% of her body mass. She can only walk with her legs wide apart, and sometimes she will dip her belly in water to soothe the inflamed skin. She has to fast for a couple of days before laying, as there is virtually no room at this time in her compressed stomach for food.

- As soon as the egg is laid, a second might already start developing, with clutch sizes reaching up to three (it can take over 50 days between the laying of the first and the third). A kiwi can lay up to 100 eggs in her lifetime.

Take Sam out of

and put the first yolk in the nest

(5 letters)
Answer on page 153

QUOTE UNQUOTE

*He seems as if his singing were a sort of talking to himself,
or of thinking aloud his strongest thoughts. I wish I was
a blackbird, like him. I hate men.*
D H Lawrence, novelist, 14 May 1915

WHY YOU SHOULD GO TO THE REUNION

Because Réunion island, in the Indian Ocean, has no fewer than
seven endemic species, which breed nowhere else.

Réunion black petrel
Réunion bulbul
Réunion cuckoo shrike
Réunion grey white-eye
Réunion olive white-eye
Réunion stonechat
Barau's petrel

Number of feathers, in thousands, on 140 ruby-throated hummingbirds 131

WHAT'S IN A NAME?

It's hard to believe that anyone could compare an ostrich with a sparrow, but the Greeks did. They even had a name for it: *struthos melage*, or big sparrow. This eventually contracted to struthion, which became the root of '-strich'. The initial 'o' is probably a contraction of 'aves', or 'bird'... presumably because in the early part of the 13th century when the ostrich was given its name, it was felt necessary to remind people that it really was a bird.

The 'os' at the beginning of osprey similarly derives from 'aves', the bird inheriting the once generic Latin title of aves praedae, or 'bird of prey'.

THE BYRDS AND THE BIRDS

Some popular music combos with avian monikers

House Martins
Buzzcocks
Counting Crows
Eagles
Blackhawk
Cock Sparrow
Flock of Seagulls
Ravens
Sandpipers
Thrashing Doves

IS IT A BIRD? IS IT A PRIMATE? IS IT A COW?

It looks like a monkey and sounds like a cross between a cow and a ship's foghorn. The capuchinbird of the Brazilian Amazon – sometimes known as the calfbird because of its mooing call – is an extraordinary looking member of the cotinga family. As it sits with its back to you in the forest branches, its smooth chestnut feathers looking for all the world like fur, you could be forgiven for thinking it was a primate. Until it turns around and looks at you with its featherless, bluish vulturine face.

Like other members of its family, it is a lekking bird. Choosing a clearing on the forest floor, a number of individuals gather, mooing in unison, sometimes in couples. Facing each other, they cock their orange-brown tail feathers, and start growling, before leaning backwards and mooing once more. Truly one of the remarkable sights of the rainforests.

BIRDBRAINERS

Which shorebird am I?
ENOTS
Answer on page 153

THE COMPLETE GUIDE TO WOODSTOCK

More than just a music gig, Woodstock is a tiny yellow bird who hangs around with Snoopy in *Peanuts* cartoons and speaks in strange scratchy marks that Snoopy can understand.

- Although birds frequently visited Snoopy's kennel in the 1960s, Woodstock wasn't named until June, 1970.
- Woodstock is reluctant to eat bread crumbs thrown out for him because he doesn't want anyone to think he's on welfare.
- Not the greatest flyer, sometimes seen wobbling through the air upside-down, he gets beak bleeds at heights above 10 feet.
- He is a fine hockey player on his iced-over birdbath, and a bit of a dab-hand at trivia games too.
- His best friends, who all look like him, are Bill, Harriet, Olivier, Raymond, Fred, Roy and Conrad.

AND YOUR BIRD CAN SING

Johnstone's lorikeet
Epaulet oriole
South Georgia diving petrel
Baringo tufted guineafowl

PHONETICALLY SPEAKING

How the Collins Bird Guide *(CBG)*, Bill Oddie's Birds of Britain and Ireland *(BOB)*, RSPB Handbook of British Birds *(HBB) and* Observer's Book of Birds *(OBB) hear the birds of parks and gardens.*

Coal tit: tih tuh-e (CBG); tsuueee (BOB); see see (HBB); if-hee (OBB)

Greenfinch: dschruuuuuh (CBG); dzweeee (BOB); dzeee (HBB); zwee (OBB)

Pied Wagtail: zi-ze-litt (CBG); 'chiswick' (BOB); chizzwit (HBB); tschis-seek (OBB)

Blackbird (alarm): pli-pli (CBG); chink chink (BOB); chink chink (HBB); pink pink (OBB)

If you've come across a place called a Ramsar site, and not known what that meant, you might have thought the word was an acronym for something. It's not. The following full definition comes from www.ramsar.org:

The Convention on Wetlands is an intergovernmental treaty adopted on 2 February 1971 in the Iranian city of Ramsar, on the southern shore of the Caspian Sea. Thus, though nowadays the name of the Convention is usually written 'Convention on Wetlands (Ramsar, Iran, 1971)', it has come to be known popularly as the 'Ramsar Convention'. Ramsar is the first of the modern global intergovernmental treaties on conservation and wise use of natural resources, but, compared with more recent ones, its provisions are relatively straightforward and general. Over the years, the Conference of the Contracting Parties (the main decision-making body of the Convention, composed of delegates from all the Member States) has further developed and interpreted the basic tenets of the treaty text and succeeded in keeping the work of the Convention abreast of changing world perceptions, priorities, and trends in environmental thinking.

The official name of the treaty – *The Convention on Wetlands of International Importance especially as Waterfowl Habitat* – reflects its original emphasis on the conservation and wise use of wetlands primarily to provide habitat for waterbirds. Over the years, however, the Convention has broadened its scope to cover all aspects of wetland conservation and wise use, recognising wetlands as ecosystems that are extremely important for biodiversity conservation in general and for the well-being of human communities. For this reason, the increasingly common use of the short form of the treaty's title, the 'Convention on Wetlands', is entirely appropriate.

The Convention entered into force in 1975 and as of September 2003 has 138 Contracting Parties. More than 1310 wetlands have been designated for inclusion in the List of Wetlands of International Importance, covering some 111 million hectares (1.11 million km2), more than the surface area of France, Germany, and Switzerland combined.

UNESCO serves as Depositary for the Convention, but its administration has been entrusted to a secretariat known as the 'Ramsar Bureau', which is housed in the headquarters of IUCN–The World Conservation Union in Gland, Switzerland, under the authority of the Conference of the Parties and the Standing Committee of the Convention.

BIRDS OF SPRINGFIELD

Bart-ailed godwit

Margelanic lesser whitethroat

DOHerty's bushshrike

Picumnus squamulatus lovejoyi (a subspecies of the scaled piculet)

Emberiza capensis smithersii (a subspecies of the cape bunting)

Plenty of Apus

NB: the only bird in the world with Homer in its name is the subspecies *Pionites leucogaster xanthomeria*. Appropriately enough for a character who has been known to offer the invitation 'kiss my hairy yellow butt', its English name is yellow-tailed caique.

QUOTE UNQUOTE

I saw [a pigeon] up on the eaves of the roof: as it moved its head a crush of satin green came and went, a wet or soft flaming of the light
Gerard Manley Hopkins, poet, 16 June 1873

TITANIC TALES

The Rhea, South America's ostrich, was named after the mythological titaness mother of Zeus by explorer Paul Mohring in 1752. Although his reasons for choosing that name are unknown, there are two interesting parallels between the bird and the esteemed goddess.

According to Greek lore, Rhea was transported by two huge chariots.

The bird has an impressive running-speed, aided by a pair of strong wings that, while not providing flight, lend considerable lift and stability.

The Greek Rhea wanted to prevent her brother, and husband, Cronus from eating their son Zeus – understandable, as he'd already wolfed down their other five children. She gave him a rock wrapped in swaddling clothes to chew on instead, and then spirited Zeus to a mountain retreat.

In a subtle role-reversal, it is the male of the feathered version who has taken on this protective instinct. If he sees any creature, whether human or even a female Rhea, approaching a clutch of new eggs, he is likely to mount a frightening charge. It is, you might say, a rhea guard action.

THE CUCKOO AND JENNERCIDE

When Edward Jenner was elected a Fellow of the Royal Society in 1789, it was for his pioneering work in smallpox vaccination which would save countless lives in the decades ahead, right? Wrong. That discovery would not be made for another seven years. He won the honour because he'd finally got to grips with the cuckoo.

The nesting habits of the bird had fooled naturalists since the days of Aristotle. Jenner was the first to show that it was not the parent bird who ejected the eggs and chicks of the host parent, as had always been thought, but the cuckoo chick itself. He discovered a depression in the chick's back which disappears after 12 days, but which by then has been used to help the chick cup and push out the foster parents' eggs.

Despite the Royal Society honour, many observers remained sceptical about the idea. It was only when 20th century photographers were actually able to film the event that Jenner was finally proved right.

ABSOLUTELY FABULOUS

The Kites and the Swans, by Aesop

The kites of olden times, as well as the swans, had the privilege of song. But having heard the neigh of the horse, they were so enchanted with the sound, that they tried to imitate it; and, in trying to neigh, they forgot how to sing.

*The desire for imaginary benefits often involves
the loss of present blessings.*

A VERY LENGTHY TALE

The onagadori, or 'honourable fowl', is the bird world's equivalent of a Crufts' all-time champion. This Japanese ornamental chicken, whose exact origins are unknown, is bred for its extravagantly long tail feathers, a practice probably reaching back to the 17th century in Shikoku Japan when the bird's feathers were used to adorn soldiers' helmets and spears in honour of the Emperor Tenno.

And how long do those feathers get? The record is truly astonishing. In 1972, a Japanese bird-fancier bred an onagadori with tail feathers reaching an almost unbelievable 10.59 metres in length. Contrast this with the longest naturally grown feathers, owned by the crested argus pheasant, which have recorded lengths of up to 1.73 metres.

Little trotty wagtail, he went in the rain,
And tittering, tottering sideways he ne'er got straight again,
He stooped to get a worm, and looked up to catch a fly,
And then he flew away ere his feathers they were dry.

Little trotty wagtail, he waddled in the mud,
And left his little footmarks, trample where he would.
And waddled in the water-pudge, and waggle went his tail,
And chirrup up his wings to dry upon the garden rail.

Little trotty wagtail, you nimble all about,
And in the dimpling water-pudge you waddle in and out;
Your home is nigh at hand, and in the warm pigsty,
So, little Master Wagtail, I'll bid you a good-bye.

John Clare (1793-1864), *Little Trotty Wagtail*

THE CUCKOO'S LINGUISTIC LEGACY

Cuckoo spit: the undigested plant sap blown out the backsides of froghopper nymphs to protect them from predators. So named because it appears as cuckoos arrive in Britain.

Cuckold: bringing home the bacon to your woman, even though she's bringing up someone else's young.

Cloudcuckooland: from Aristophanes' play *The Birds*, in which this avian city in the sky is built by two Athenians as a perfect paradise, but ends up becoming just as bad as the Athens they tried to leave behind.

Cuckoo's nest: a hornpipe, and (intriguingly) a Brighton-based women's morris dancing group. Intriguing because the meaning of cuckoo's nest can be found in the following lyrics:

> *As I was a walkin' one morning in May*
> *I met a pretty fair maid and unto her did say,*
> *For love I'm inclined*
> *And I'll tell you me mind*
> *That me inclination lies in your cuckoo's nest*

> *Some like a girl who is pretty in the face,*
> *And some like a girl who is slender in the waist,*
> *But I like a girl*
> *Who will wriggle and will twist*
> *At the bottom of the belly lies the cuckoo's nest.*

All the people appear in the temples in white garments; but the priest's vestments are parti-coloured, and both the work and colours are wonderful. They are made of no rich materials, for they are neither embroidered nor set with precious stones; but are composed of the plumes of several birds, laid together with so much art, and so neatly, that the true value of them is far beyond the costliest materials. They say, that in the ordering and placing those plumes some dark mysteries are represented, which pass down among their priests in a secret tradition concerning them; and that they are as hieroglyphics, putting them in mind of the blessing that they have received from God, and of their duties, both to Him and to their neighbours. As soon as the priest appears in those ornaments, they all fall prostrate on the ground, with so much reverence and so deep a silence, that such as look on cannot but be struck with it, as if it were the effect of the appearance of a deity.

Sir Thomas More, *Utopia*, 1516

BIRD CAKE RECIPE. SERVES DOZENS

Melt one part lard or solid vegetable fat, and mix in two parts of a mixture of seeds, raisins and porridge oats.

Put the mixture while still warm in an empty milk carton.

Drape piece of string into mixture, leaving a length of about 10 inches lying loose.

Allow to cool until solid.

Hang from bird table.

Serve with water bowl.

Retreat to window and watch.

ON A TREE BY A RIVER...

In March 1885, the newest offering from the popular music combo Gilbert and Sullivan opened at the Savoy, London, and enjoyed a successful run of 672 performances. Audiences to *The Mikado* particularly loved the ditty 'Tit-willow', a maudlin little tale sung by Ko-Ko to represent his own sense of frustrated love.

Yet Gilbert's lyrics were strangely prescient (even though the bird he was writing about was the tom-tit, or blue tit). Just 15 years after the operetta's debut, a new species was discovered by science. The willow tit, previously thought to be a sub-species of the marsh tit, was separated from its cousin in 1900, its most distinguishing feature in the field being... its call.

ABSOLUTELY FABULOUS

The Fighting Cocks and the Eagle, by Aesop

Two gamecocks were fiercely fighting for the mastery of the farmyard. One at last put the other to flight. The vanquished cock skulked away and hid himself in a quiet corner, while the conqueror, flying up to a high wall, flapped his wings and crowed exultingly with all his might. An eagle sailing through the air pounced upon him and carried him off in his talons. The vanquished cock immediately came out of his corner, and ruled henceforth with undisputed mastery.

Pride goes before a fall

THE RETURN OF THE RED KITE

1989 The reintroduction programme begins, as 93 birds from Spain and Sweden start to be released in Buckinghamshire and north Scotland.

1995 70 further kites are released in the east Midlands over three years.

1996 19 further birds are brought from Germany to central Scotland.

1999 At least 20 further European birds are released near Leeds.

2001 Another 19 kites take wing in Dumfries and Galloway.

2004 20 Oxfordshire birds are captured and set free near Gateshead. In this year, the Chiltern birds alone produced over 200 chicks.

QUOTE UNQUOTE

'Do you know,' Peter asked, 'why swallows build in the eaves of houses? It is to listen to the stories.'
JM Barrie, *Peter Pan*

DEATH FROM THE SKIES

What's more threatening than a tyrannosaur?
A tyrannosaur that can fly.

Fortunately for Rex's Cretaceous contemporaries, he could do no such thing, but evidence has recently revealed that his ancestors did at least have feathers. *Dilong paradoxus* was an early tyrannosauroid (around 130 myo, some 60 million years older than *Tyrannosaurus rex*), that has recently been uncovered in China, and found to have had protofeathers on its tail and jaw. Current thinking is that the feathers were for insulation rather than flight, and as tyrannosaurs grew over the years they steadily shed them.

I wanna marabou, isn't that what you want too?
BB King/Eric Clapton

BIRDBRAINERS

What kind of duck am I?
Branta without the last letter, plus the Queen
Answer on page 153

THE STORIES BEHIND THE
BIRDS OF HOLLYWOOD

Daphne du Maurier's tale *The Birds* was markedly changed by Hitchcock for his film of the same name, the master of suspense ignoring virtually everything except the central concept of avian attacks. But in 2001, 38 years after the film was released, the theme was handed back rather dramatically to the du Maurier family.

Seagull attacks have become more frequent along various parts of the British coastline in recent years, and in May 2001 a Cornishman reported that he and his wife were being terrorised by gulls nesting outside their cottage. It turned out that he was Christian Browning, du Maurier's son.

To the Japanese the crane is a symbol of peace, and has been since the 11th century feudal warlord, Yoshiye, released hundreds of them with paper strips tied to their legs in memory of those who had fallen in battle. From this action a legend steadily grew: fold one thousand origami cranes, and the gods will grant you your most peaceful wish.

After the second world war, scarred by the years of battle and the horror of atomic warfare, Japan was in severe need of peace. One small girl, Sadako Sasaki, a resident of Hiroshima, had contracted leukaemia from the nuclear fallout of the Allies' brutal ending of the war, and she vowed to make one thousand paper cranes in her own personal quest for world peace. Her efforts did not go unnoticed, and when, as a teenager, the disease claimed her in 1955 still 355 birds short, her schoolfriends finished her project and erected the Tower of a Thousand Cranes in her memory in the city's Peace Memorial Park. To this day the people of Hiroshima still keep adding their own cranes, fashioned from brightly coloured paper, to the tower.

ANNUAL SALES OF THE OBSERVER'S BOOK OF BIRDS IN THE FINAL YEARS

1974	95,500
1975	83,939
1976	81,665
1977	66,428
1978	60,438
1979	56,488
1980	45,623
1981	25,344

The book's peak decade was in the 1960s,
when it sold 1,040,400 copies.

WHAT'S IN A NAME?

Look up the word godwit in most dictionaries, and you'll find that it's of uncertain origin. One theory, however, is that it is derived from the middle English good wight, meaning good person or good fellow. This wasn't in reference to its personality, nor to the folklore character Robin Goodfellow, but to the fact that godwits made very tasty dishes at mediaeval banquets. The bird's generic name (*Limosa*) is easier to source: *limosus* is Latin for mud.

[Ethelberta] looked up and saw a wild-duck flying along with the greatest violence, just in its rear being another large bird, which a countryman would have pronounced to be one of the biggest duck-hawks that he had ever beheld. The hawk neared its intended victim, and the duck screamed and redoubled its efforts.

Ethelberta impulsively started off in a rapid run that would have made a little dog bark with delight and run after, her object being, if possible, to see the end of this desperate struggle for a life so small and unheard-of...

Her rate of advance was not to be compared with that of the two birds, though she went swiftly enough to keep them well in sight in such an open place as that around her, having at one point in the journey been so near that she could hear the whisk of the duck's feathers against the wind as it lifted and lowered its wings. When the bird seemed to be but a few yards from its enemy she saw it strike downwards, and after a level flight of a quarter of a minute, vanish. The hawk swooped after, and Ethelberta now perceived a whitely shining oval of still water, looking amid the swarthy level of the heath like a hole through to a nether sky.

Into this large pond, which the duck had been making towards from the beginning of its precipitate flight, it had dived out of sight. The excited and breathless runner was in a few moments close enough to see the disappointed hawk hovering and floating in the air as if waiting for the reappearance of its prey, upon which grim pastime it was so intent that by creeping along softly she was enabled to get very near the edge of the pool and witness the conclusion of the episode. Whenever the duck was under the necessity of showing its head to breathe, the other bird would dart towards it, invariably too late, however; for the diver was far too experienced in the rough humour of the buzzard family at this game to come up twice near the same spot, unaccountably emerging from opposite sides of the pool in succession, and bobbing again by the time its adversary reached each place, so that at length the hawk gave up the contest and flew away, a satanic moodiness being almost perceptible in the motion of its wings.

Thomas Hardy, *The Hand of Ethelberta*, 1875/6

QUOTE UNQUOTE

If one cannot catch the bird of paradise, better take a wet hen.
Nikita Kruschev
Former Premier, Soviet Union

ALL CHANGE?

In his 1951 *New Naturalist* book *Birds and Men*, ornithologist Max Nicholson called for a change in seven birds' names:

Hedge sparrow	*to*	Dunnock
Song thrush	*to*	Throstle
Great spotted woodpecker	*to*	Pied woodpecker
Lesser spotted woodpecker	*to*	Barred woodpecker
Great black-backed gull	*to*	Great blackback
Lesser black-backed gull	*to*	Lesser blackback
Common gull	*to*	Mew gull

To date, only the first of his list has been accepted.

ONLY A POOR LITTLE SPARROW

When Chaucer spoke of the humble 'sparwe', which species was he talking about? Who can say. In Chaucer's day there was only one known sparrow: the tree sparrow was not formally recognised as a separate species until 1713.

ROBIN DEADBREAST

When the first British settlers landed in the New World, they immediately set about nostalgically naming places and wildlife after their own native favourites. Thus it was that the first songbird they saw hopping about with a red breast became the American robin, despite the fact it was a thrush.

And one American robin discovered the tough life of the Old World for itself, when it arrived in Grimsby in 2004 after a misdirected transatlantic flight, and settled in to make the east coast of England its home. It was, naturally enough for such an unusual visitor, besieged by twitchers… and fate. Two months after its arrival, it was snatched from in front of the cameras and binoculars by a sparrowhawk.

ABSOLUTELY FABULOUS

The Hawk, the Kite, and the Pigeons, by Aesop
The pigeons, terrified by the appearance of a kite, called upon the hawk to defend them. He at once consented. When they had admitted him into the cote, they found that he made more havoc and slew a larger number of them in one day than the kite could pounce upon in a whole year.

Avoid a remedy that is worse than the disease

Weighed down upon the swanny river
Florida state song

QUOTE UNQUOTE

*I know of only one bird – the parrot – that talks;
and it can't fly very high.*
Wilbur Wright, early aviator, on his reasons for
declining giving a speech

FRATERCUTAH ARCTICA

Which bird once sounded as if it should be living in Salt Lake City?
The answer is the puffin, which in the 19th century was popularly
known as the mormon. Yet there was no religious connotation to this
name; it was a derivation from mormo, the Greek for hobgoblin.

The bird swam swiftly and gracefully toward the Magic Isle, and as it drew nearer its gorgeously coloured plumage astonished them. The feathers were of many hues of glistening greens and blues and purples, and it had a yellow head with a red plume, and pink, white and violet in its tail. When it reached the Isle, it came ashore and approached them, waddling slowly and turning its head first to one side and then to the other, so as to see the girl and the sailor better.

'You're strangers,' said the bird, coming to a halt near them, 'and you've been caught by the Magic Isle and made prisoners.'

'Yes,' returned Trot, with a sigh; 'we're rooted. But I hope we won't grow.'

'You'll grow small,' said the Bird. 'You'll keep growing smaller every day, until bye and bye there'll be nothing left of you. That's the usual way, on this Magic Isle.'

'How do you know about it, and who are you, anyhow?' asked Cap'n Bill.

'I'm the Lonesome Duck,' replied the bird. 'I suppose you've heard of me?'

'No,' said Trot, 'I can't say I have. What makes you lonesome?'

'Why, I haven't any family or any relations,' returned the Duck.

'Haven't you any friends?'

'Not a friend. And I've nothing to do. I've lived a long time, and I've got to live forever, because I belong in the Land of Oz, where no living thing dies. Think of existing year after year, with no friends, no family, and nothing to do! Can you wonder I'm lonesome?'

'Why don't you make a few friends, and find something to do?' inquired Cap'n Bill.

'I can't make friends because everyone I meet – bird, beast, or person – is disagreeable to me. In a few minutes I shall be unable to bear your society longer, and then I'll go away and leave you,' said the Lonesome Duck. 'And, as for doing anything, there's no use in it. All I meet are doing something, so I have decided it's common and uninteresting and I prefer to remain lonesome.'

'Don't you have to hunt for your food?' asked Trot.

'No. In my diamond palace, a little way up the river, food is magically supplied me; but I seldom eat, because it is so common.'

'You must be a Magician Duck,' remarked Cap'n Bill.

'Why so?'

'Well, ordinary ducks don't have diamond palaces an' magic food, like you do.'

'True; and that's another reason why I'm lonesome. You must remember I'm the only Duck in the Land of Oz, and I'm not like any other duck in the outside world.'

'Seems to me you LIKE bein' lonesome,' observed Cap'n Bill.

'I can't say I like it, exactly,' replied the Duck, 'but since it seems to be my fate, I'm rather proud of it.'

'How do you s'pose a single, solitary Duck happened to be in the Land of Oz?' asked Trot, wonderingly.

'I used to know the reason, many years ago, but I've quite forgotten it,' declared the Duck. 'The reason for a thing is never so important as the thing itself, so there's no use remembering anything but the fact that I'm lonesome.'

'I guess you'd be happier if you tried to do something,' asserted Trot. 'If you can't do anything for yourself, you can do things for others, and then you'd get lots of friends and stop being lonesome.'

'Now you're getting disagreeable,' said the Lonesome Duck, 'and I shall have to go and leave you.'

'Can't you help us any?' pleaded the girl. 'If there's anything magic about you, you might get us out of this scrape.'

'I haven't any magic strong enough to get you off the Magic Isle,' replied the Lonesome Duck. 'What magic I possess is very simple, but I find it enough for my own needs.'

'If we could only sit down a while, we could stand it better,' said Trot, 'but we have nothing to sit on.'

'Then you will have to stand it,' said the Lonesome Duck.

'P'raps you've enough magic to give us a couple of stools,' suggested Cap'n Bill.

'A duck isn't supposed to know what stools are,' was the reply.

'But you're diff'rent from all other ducks.'

'That is true.' The strange creature seemed to reflect for a moment, looking at them sharply from its round black eyes. Then it said: 'Sometimes, when the sun is hot, I grow a toadstool to shelter me from its rays. Perhaps you could sit on toadstools.'

'Well, if they were strong enough, they'd do,' answered Cap'n Bill.

'Then, before I go I'll give you a couple,' said the Lonesome Duck, and began waddling about in a small circle. It went around the circle to the right three times, and then it went around to the left three times. Then it hopped backward three times and forward three times.

...The sailor-man felt something touch him from behind and, turning his head, he found a big toadstool in just the right place and of just the right size to sit upon. There was one behind Trot, too, and with a cry of pleasure the little girl sank back upon it and found it a very comfortable seat – solid, yet almost like a cushion. 'Thank you, ever so much!' cried Trot, and the sailor called out: 'Much obliged!'

But the Lonesome Duck paid no attention. Without even looking in their direction again, the gaudy fowl entered the water and swam gracefully away.

L Frank Baum, *The Magic of Oz*

BUDGE UP

Legend would have us believe that the word budgerigar is derived from an old aboriginal word meaning 'good food', though this almost certainly started as a mischievous joke when the Aborigines met their first ignorant Europeans. More likely, though less amusing, is the theory that the word translates as 'good bird'... begging the question, good for what?

A GOLDCREST BY ANY OTHER NAME

Regional names for the goldcrest include:

Golden cutty	*Hampshire*
Tidley goldfinch	*Devon*
Wood titmouse	*Cornwall*
Moonie	*Roxburgh*
Thumb bird	*Hampshire*
Tot o'erseas	*East Anglia*
Woodcock pilot	*Yorkshire*
Herring Spink	*Suffolk*

QUOTE UNQUOTE

I planted some bird seed. A bird came up.
Now I don't know what to feed it.
Steven Wright, comedian

FOWLES PLAY

Once, in Crete, I was climbing a mountain alone. Heavy snowdrifts made me give up the attempt to reach the top, but before I began the descent I lay down on my back between two boulders in order to rest out of the icy wind. A minute passed. Then, with an abruptness that stopped my breath, I was not alone. A huge winged shape was hanging in the air some twenty feet above my head. It looked like an enormous falcon, its great wings feathering and flexed to the wind current, a savage hooked beak tilted down at me. I lay as still as stone, like Sinbad under the roc. For some ten seconds the great bird and I were transfixed, in a kind of silent dialogue. I knew it was a lammergeier, one of Europe's largest birds of prey – a species few ornithologists have seen in the wild at all, let alone from a few feet away. Ten seconds, and then it decided I was alive and swung a mile away in one great sweep on rigid wings.

John Fowles, *The Blinded Eye*,
published in *Animals*,
January 1971

What am I?
GLEKT
Answer on page 153

WINGED WORDS

Although in oceanic islands the number of kinds of inhabitants is scanty, the proportion of endemic species (ie those found nowhere else in the world) is often extremely large. If we compare, for instance, the number of the endemic land-shells in Madeira, or of the endemic birds in the Galapagos Archipelago, with the number found on any continent, and then compare the area of the islands with that of the continent, we shall see that this is true. This fact might have been expected on my theory for, as already explained, species occasionally arriving after long intervals in a new and isolated district, and having to compete with new associates, will be eminently liable to modification, and will often produce groups of modified descendants. But it by no means follows, that, because in an island nearly all the species of one class are peculiar, those of another class, or of another section of the same class, are peculiar; and this difference seems to depend on the species which do not become modified having immigrated with facility and in a body, so that their mutual relations have not been much disturbed. Thus in the Galapagos Islands nearly every land-bird, but only two out of the eleven marine birds, are peculiar; and it is obvious that marine birds could arrive at these islands more easily than land-birds. Bermuda, on the other hand, which lies at about the same distance from North America as the Galapagos Islands do from South America, and which has a very peculiar soil, does not possess one endemic land bird; and we know from Mr J M Jones's admirable account of Bermuda, that very many North American birds, during their great annual migrations, visit either periodically or occasionally this island. Madeira does not possess one peculiar bird, and many European and African birds are almost every year blown there, as I am informed by Mr E V Harcourt. So that these two islands of Bermuda and Madeira have been stocked by birds, which for long ages have struggled together in their former homes, and have become mutually adapted to each other; and when settled in their new homes, each kind will have been kept by the others to their proper places and habits, and will consequently have been little liable to modification.

Charles Darwin,
The Origin of Species

WHAT'S IN A NAME?

Sometimes those who name birds try to get a little too clever. The ptarmigan derived its name from the Gaelic tarmachen, or mountaineer – simple enough. But in 1684, some wise guy put a 'p' in front of it, thinking the name came from the Greek ptarmike, or yellow (the birds can look a little off-white in a certain light). The redundant letter is still with us today.

GAME BIRDS

Confused by cardinals? Bewildered by blackhawks? Here's a handy guide to the major American sports teams with avian monikers.

Baseball
Saint Louis Cardinals
Toronto Blue Jays

Basketball
Atlanta Hawks
Toronto Raptors

Football
Atlanta Falcons
Baltimore Ravens
Philadelphia Eagles
Seattle Seahawks
Arizona Cardinals

Ice hockey
Chicago Blackhawks
Anaheim Mighty Ducks
Pittsburgh Penguins

THROUGH WHITE'S EYES

Birds as observed by Gilbert White in his *Natural History of Selborne*, 1788/9

The blue titmouse, or nun, is a great frequenter of houses, and a general devourer. Beside insects, it is very fond of flesh; for it frequently picks bones on dung-hills: it is a vast admirer of suet, and haunts butchers' shops. When a boy, I have known twenty in a morning caught with snap mousetraps, baited with tallow or suet. It will also pick holes in apples left on the ground, and be well entertained with the seeds on the head of a sunflower. The blue, marsh, and great titmice will, in very severe weather, carry away barley and oat straws from the sides of ricks.

A SHRIKE IN TIME SAVES NINE

An old English term for shrikes was nine-killer, based on the belief that the bird stocked up its larder by killing nine birds daily to impale on its spikes.

THE BIRDER WHO CAME IN FROM THE COLD

Rumours about the origins of the term twitcher abound. There's the theory that the word is connected to the behaviour of the thrilled enthusiast on sighting an anticipated rarity; then there's the idea that in the pre-pager days, keenos started to get a bit 'twitchy' if the wind was coming from a particular direction at the relevant time of year. Another thought is that 'twitching' was an amalgamation of the words 'ticking' and 'watching', combining the twitcher's most common activities.

Yet the most delightful version of this word's etymology is that it was coined by birdwatchers John Izzard and Bob Emmett in the 1950s, to describe their friend Howard Medhurst. To reach the location of a reported sighting, the trio would drive the length and breadth of the country, Howard riding pillion on Bob's Matchless 350 Motorbike. On arrival at some distant destination, Howard would stagger off the back of the bike, so frozen by the journey that all he could do was twitch and shiver with cold. This performance was repeated so regularly up and down the country that John and Bob began to refer to the birdwatching pilgrimages as 'being on a twitch'.

QUOTE UNQUOTE

When your pet bird sees you reading the newspaper, does he think you are just sitting there staring at carpeting?
Anon

WINGED WORDS

There are a few sounds still which never fail to affect me. The notes of the wood thrush and the sound of a vibrating chord, these affect me as many sounds once did often, and as almost all should. The strains of the aeolian harp and of the wood thrush are the truest and loftiest preachers that I know now left on earth. I know of no missionaries to us heathen comparable to them. They, as it were, lift us up in spite of ourselves. They intoxicate, they charm us.
Henry David Thoreau, *Journal*, 31 December 1853

Was invaded by waxwings first, twitchers second

Discovered that a nibble of bird seed cake is a nibble too much

Picked up five lifers in Shetland and three hitch-hikers
on the way back

Got pretty darn good at imitating a wood full of tawny owls

Dipped on a dipper

Contemplated the sun reflecting off a kingfisher's back and wondered
if anything could be more wonderful

Made like a jacana across the desk-tops and stubbed three toes

Decided that the simplicity and control of the swift's flight beat the
kingfisher into second place

Saw or heard 89 species in one day, then revised the total to 88 owing
to the somewhat suspicious midday tawny owl

Visited the Bird Fair, spent far more than intended, and joined three
organisations never previously heard of

On at least 20 occasions raised the bins quickly only to find
it was a pigeon

Wished to have been there, like Gilbert White, in the early days when
there was so much still to discover, then realised that there will always
be more to discover than can be achieved in any one lifetime, no
matter which century we live in

*Please note that although every effort has been made to ensure
accuracy in this book, the above statistics may be the result of
fowled-up minds.*

In few if any other large countries and at no other period could the present scale and variety of human impact on bird life in Britain be matched, and in no other country is there, or has there been, so widespread an informed interest in birds

Max Nicholson, 1951

The Answers. In case you were a silly goose and didn't get them all.

P11.   Tit for tat

P20.   They are the scientific names of the Laurel pigeon and Hardy's pygmy-owl

P23.   Coot (The pictured bird is the o'o)

P28.   Hobby

P37.   Aniseed (The pictured bird is the ani)

P41.   Plover (P + lover)

P44.   Jay (10th letter of the alphabet)

P46.   Greenshank (Rook – oo, shag, nene)

P52.   Can't see the wood for the trees (Woodhoopoe – hoopoe)

P55.   Bee-eater

P59.   Partridge

P69.   Flamingo

P76.   Manx shearwater (*Puffinus puffinus*)

P78.   Shoehorn (Shoebill and hornbill)

P83.   Francolin

P91.   Smote (Titmouse – tui = tmose, then rearrange)

P92.   Cardinal

P103. Hawfinch

P107. Pigeon (Wigeon – w + p)

P110. Axing (Waxwing – ww)

P116. The semaphore reads 'Icky Cley'

P120. Crossbill

P126. Treecreeper

P131. Eyrie (The pictured bird is a seriema)

P133. Turnstone

P140. Goosander (Goose – e and ER)

P148. Kinglet

We look to birds for a very deep-seated kind of joy. It goes back to the dawn of humankind: ever since humans first walked upright, they were able to turn their eyes to the heavens and observe the birds.

Simon Barnes

ACKNOWLEDGEMENTS

We gratefully acknowledge permission to reprint extracts of copyright material in this book from the following authors, publishers and executors:

How To Be A Bad Birdwatcher by Simon Barnes by kind permission of Short Books.

Copyright ©, *Birders: Tales of a Tribe* by Mark Cocker, published by Jonathan Cape, by kind permission of Rogers, Coleridge & White.

The Blinded Eye, John Fowles, Copyright © John Fowles by permission of Gillon Aitken Associates.

Excerpt from *Gujarat and Rajasthan* from *The Birds of Heaven* by Peter Matthiesen. Copyright © 2001 by Peter Matthiessen. Reprinted by permission of North Point Press, a division of Farra, Strauss and Giroux, LLC.

Extract from *The Birds of Heaven: Travels with Cranes* by Peter Matthiesen published by The Harvill Press. Used by permission of The Random House Group Limited.

From *Nature's Child: Encounters with Wonders of the Natural World* by John Lister-Kaye. Copyright © John Lister-Kaye 2004, published by Little, Brown, an imprint of Time Warner Book Group UK. Reproduced by permission of Felicity Bryan Literary Agency and the author.

March from *A Country Calendar and Other Writings* by Thompson, Flora edited by Lane, Margaret (1979) By permission of Oxford University Press.

Number of birds, in thousands, that over-winter at the Thames Estuary and 155
Marshes Special Protection Area

Since 1946, when Sir Peter Scott chose Slimbridge, on the Severn Estuary in Gloucestershire, as the headquarters of the Wildfowl & Wetlands Trust, the charity has opened a door to the wonderful world of wetlands, their birds and other wildlife for millions of visitors across Britain and the world.

Nearly 60 years on, nine visitor centres and a whole team of researchers drive WWT forward in its aim to save wetlands for wildlife and people. With half of the world's precious wetlands, from ponds and lakes to rivers and their floodplains, marshes, swamps and coastal waters lost over the last 100 years, and 45 species and subspecies of waterfowl threatened with extinction worldwide, this work is now more important than ever.

WWT is perhaps best known for the Bewick's and whooper swans that spend the winter months in many of its centres. In fact, the organisation's logo features one of each of these majestic birds. Since the 1960s when Sir Peter Scott discovered that each individual Bewick's swan can be identified by its unique bill pattern, swan research has been at the forefront of WWT's work. A visit to Slimbridge, Martin Mere, Welney, Caerlaverock or the National Wetlands Centre Wales from November to February offers the experience of one of winter's very best wildlife spectacles: masses of migratory swans.

Each season at WWT centres holds the promise of something new and exciting. From breeding waders, ducks and geese in the spring, to flamingo chicks in the summer months, breathtaking autumn wader passages and, of course, a healthy share of rarities blowing in on a good wind, a visit to a WWT centre is a must for birders and non-birders alike.

All WWT's work is underpinned by its members. Each membership helps to fund the charity's valuable worldwide conservation work.

To find out more, visit the website www.wwt.org.uk or call the membership office on 01453 891915.

INDEX

The Birdwatcher's Companion Twitchers, birders, ornithologists and garden-tickers: there are many species of birdwatcher, and you're all catered for by this unique book. ISBN 1-86105-833-0

The Cook's Companion Whether your taste is for foie gras or fry-ups, this tasty compilation is an essential ingredient in any kitchen, boiling over with foodie fact and fiction. ISBN 1-86105-772-5

The Gardener's Companion For anyone who has ever put on a pair of gloves, picked up a spade and gone out into the garden in search of flowers, beauty and inspiration. ISBN 1-86105-771-7

The Golfer's Companion Bogeys and shanking, plus fours and six irons, the alleged etiquette of caddies – all you need to know about the heaven and hell of golf is in this unique book. ISBN 1-86105-834-9

The Ideas Companion This fascinating book tells the stories behind the trademarks, inventions, and brands that we come across every day. ISBN 1-86105-835-7

The Legal Companion From lawmakers to lawbreakers, this fascinating compilation offers a view of the oddities, quirks, origins and stories behind the legal world. ISBN 1-86105-838-1

The Literary Companion Whether your Dickens is Charles or Monica, your Stein Gertrude or Franken, here's your book. Literary fact and fiction from Rebecca East to Vita Sackville-West. ISBN 1-86105-798-9

The London Companion From Edgware to Mörden, Upminster to Ealing, here's your chance to explore the history and mystery of the most exciting capital city in the world. ISBN 1-86105-799-7

The Moviegoer's Companion Explore the strange and wonderful world of movies, actors, cinemas and salty popcorn in all their glamorous glory from film noir to Matt LeBlanc. ISBN 1-86105-797-0

The Politics Companion The history, myths, great leaders and greater liars of international politics are all gathered around the hustings in this remarkable compilation. ISBN 1-86105-796-2

The Sailing Companion This is the book for everyone who knows their starboard from their stinkpot, and their Raggie from their stern – and anybody who wants to find out. ISBN 1-86105-839-X

The Traveller's Companion For anyone who's ever stared at a distant plane, wondered where it's going, and spent the rest of the day dreaming of faraway lands. ISBN 1-86105-773-3

The Walker's Companion If you've ever laced a sturdy boot, packed a cheese sandwich, and stepped out in search of stimulation and contemplation, then this book is for you. ISBN 1-86105-825-X

The Wildlife Companion Animal amazements, ornithological oddities and botanical beauties abound in this compilation of natural need-to-knows and nonsense for wildlife-lovers. ISBN 1-86105-770-9